Composing Useful Pasts

History as Contemporary Politics

Edited by
EDMUND E. JACOBITTI

State University of New York Press

Chapter One is a revised version of a chapter from *Tropes of Politics*, Nelson, John S. © 1998. Reprinted by permission of The University of Wisconsin Press.

Chapter Two is from *History Made, History Imagined.* Copyright 1999 by the Board of Trustees of the University of Illinois. Used with the permission of the University of Illinois Press.

Published by
State University of New York Press, Albany

For information, address State University of New York Press,
90 State Street, Suite 700, Albany, NY 12207

Production, Laurie Searl
Marketing, Patrick Durocher

Library of Congress Cataloging-in-Publication Data

Composing useful pasts : history as contemporary politics / edited by Edmund E. Jacobitti.
p. cm.
Includes bibliographical references and index.
ISBN 0-7914-4675-1 (alk. paper) — ISBN 0-7914-4676-X (pbk. : alk paper)
1. History—Philosophy. 2. Historiography. 3. Truth. 4. Politics, Practical. I. Jacobitti, Edmund E., 1938–
D16.9.C625 2000
901—dc21 99-088325

10 9 8 7 6 5 4 3 2 1

Contents

Illustrations

Preface

In his study of the United Nations relief operation in Cambodia,[1] William Shawcross reported that, at the beginning of his research into the administration of the program, he inquired for the "Historical Office of the United Nations." To his amazement, he found that in that whole enormous complex of offices, archives, and records, there was no such place. "There is no historian at the United Nations," he learned, "because no two members here could possibly agree on what has happened, let alone on what should be recorded."[2]

The response of the traditional historian—and for that matter the response of almost any educated person—to such disagreement would probably be that consensus is impossible only because the various delegations to the United Nations are not truly interested in history but only in compiling a list of accumulated grudges to justify their contemporary interests. If people set aside those interests and grievances and dispassionately examined the record, agreement could be achieved. Indeed, once agreement about the past was attained, even present conflicts would disappear; for the record would reveal legitimate wrongs and open the door to a redress of such grievances. In short, the historical facts are "back there," somewhere, and objective historians and disinterested investigators can find them.

The essays in this volume take a different point of view. They hold that the facts are not "back there." In fact, historical "facts" only arise in the present and are designed to serve present interests. History, therefore, is not a "settled" record of the dead past, but a poetic or imaginative creation stimulated by and focused on contemporary interests. As the Italian historian Benedetto Croce put it, "the practical need is at the bottom of every historical judgement and confers upon every history the character of contemporary history. Even though the facts that pertain may seem chronologically distant or very remote, in reality history always refers to the needs of the present situation."[3]

History, in short, is always and necessarily a selective interpretation of events, an interpretation that arises only because of some pressing question in the present; and that question can only be answered in terms that address the interests, concerns, and problems of contemporary readers. The past, therefore, takes on a different meaning to different investigators and lends itself to different explanations as present interests unfold. Like events and interests in our own past, those in history acquire different meanings and require different interpretations as time passes. The essays in this volume do not permit one to assume that any final resolution or interpretation of the meaning of history (or even an individual life) will occur. Interpretations will constantly change because the interpreters stand always in the midst of history. Like characters in a novel, they are unable to escape the text and become "objective readers."

One reason historical accounts differ is that they are the product of a person's or a people's distinctive cultural personality, the language in which they express their identity and interests in an ever-changing present. A person or a people that has set aside its present concerns is a people that has surrendered its identity. Such self-abnegation is not unknown, but it is always a traumatic and often a fatal episode. Moreover, even if it were possible to measure different peoples according to a standard that eschews their local religious, cultural, and political interests in favor of abstract, universal, and eternal values, such a universal ideal conceals a very troubling vision, that of humans as carbon copies, all ideally sharing—or forced to share—the same truth. Instead, we argue, that a people are their interests; and it is only to be expected that a healthy people will create, defend, and continually update their respective pasts in accord with their changing present needs. Historical accounts, therefore, will always differ in time and space and should be seen as part of the contemporary political struggle of interests. As the various United Nations delegations rightly saw, "historical accounts" are arguments, "fighting words," that justify and vindicate present political and cultural interests. Unanimity about the past, in short, might well eliminate conflict in the present, but only by eliminating all but one view. To accept the received historical explanation of the present, in other words, is to submit to the present historical situation. To change the present requires revising the past.

To establish the origins of a historical event is a difficult task. It is also, as every writer knows, difficult to establish the origin of a text. One of the generative moments of this work occurred years ago when I began teaching. Early on, in a Junior level history class, I asked what the students thought of the interpretation a certain text had given to the French Revolution of 1789. Having diligently prepared for a question about names, dates, and battles, the students found this query utterly mysterious, as if I had stupidly asked what they thought about a column of numbers or the color of elephants. Finally, after some nervous glances and an embarrassed shuffling of feet one student, replying with a "the-sky-is-blue" shrug, observed, "Well, it's just a history book isn't it?"

That reply, so obvious to them and supported by polite, if furtive, nods of approval rather startled me. Fresh from graduate school where "interpretation" seemed to be the only question, I had wandered onto another court, one ruled by "basketball-coach-historians" who equated interpretation with a fuzzy memory. In this court, one did not "interpret" historical facts. One looked them up somewhere where they were arranged in an orderly list; and then one memorized the list.

I was surprised at this because American students, even if they might not fully understand the implications of relativism, were remarkably willing to accept the fact that different peoples, cultures, and individuals viewed the world differently. Having a point of view, a vested interest, or a motive, seemed natural to them. But having a point of view about the past seemed like having a "point of view" about the president's birthday or who won the World Series in 1950. It seemed, in short, to contradict the well-accepted maxim that "hindsight is twenty-twenty." But, in fact, because the past and the present are woven together, there is very little, of significance anyway, that is settled or agreed upon in history.

The five essays in this volume, together with the introduction, are designed to show advanced undergraduates and graduate students in the humanities or social sciences the power of historical explanation in contemporary political life. Precisely because "history" is a rhetorical and political argument about the present, individuals should not submit uncritically to such accounts. These essays should make students aware of the importance of articulating and defending their own historical arguments against other inimical accounts. Simply because some historical accounts are absurd power plays, in other words, is no reason to think they will not be successful. Indeed, unless they are countered with different histories, they *will* be successful.

NOTES

1. *The Quality of Mercy: Cambodia, Holocaust, and Modern Conscience* (New York: Simon and Schuster, 1984).

2. As quoted in Shirley Hazzard, "Breaking Faith-II," *The New Yorker*, October 2, 1989, 74–96, 94.

3. *La storia come pensiero e come azione*, my translation (Bari: Laterza, 1966), 11.

Acknowledgments

Every author, of course, has been asked the inevitable, "How long did it take you to write the book?" The only reply I ever heard that made any sense was "all my life plus the time it took to type it." That being the case, every author accumulates a lot of intellectual debts. In my own case, it would be impossible to thank everyone who has read the various stages of this manuscript on its journey to press. As editor, I probably exasperated more people than the individual authors here included; for having already inflicted the introductory essay on my family, friends, and colleagues, I asked each of the contributors to read my essay to see if they wanted to risk appearing in its wake and suffering the collateral damage. So, to each of them I here acknowledge my thankful appreciation. To my wife Suzanne, who read my essay almost as often as I did and without whose valuable criticism the book would never have been completed, I can only say I will try to do shorter projects in the future.

To my colleagues, Charles B. Anderson, Stephen Brown, John Nelson, John Paul Russo, Vickie Sullivan, as well as to the anonymous readers at SUNY, who read my introduction and made so many helpful suggestions, I owe a special debt of gratitude. It is said that when you want something done, ask a busy person. These busy people went beyond mere collegiality and I shall always remember and value their help.

INTRODUCTION

The Role of the Past in Contemporary Political Life

Edmund E. Jacobitti

The Nature of Poetic Understanding

In his novel *Ragtime*, E.L. Doctorow detailed an encounter between the anarchist Emma Goldman (1869–1940) and the beautiful socialite Evelyn Helen Nesbit (1884–1967) whose husband, Henry K. Thaw, rocked the New York social set in 1906 by murdering his wife's alleged lover, Stanford White. When Doctorow was asked if the two women had ever really had such an encounter, he replied, "They have now." Mixing fact and fiction has always, of course, been acceptable practice in novels, even historical novels. Since the time of Plato's metaphor of the cave,[1] however, the aim of reason and philosophy has been to escape the shadowy fictional world. Today, however, the border between fact and fiction has broken down. As Gordon Wood recently lamented, "The blurring of fact and fiction is part of the intellectual climate of our postmodern time—dominated as it is by winds of epistemological skepticism and Nietzschean denials of the possibility of objectivity that are sweeping through every humanistic discipline."[2]

The particular object of Wood's ire at that point was Simon Schama, the famous Harvard historian who with many others[3] has become skeptical about the possibility of objective social science and has found more fertile ground in the marriage of history and imaginative narrative. Thus, in introducing *Citizens: A Chronicle of the French Revolution*, his monumental 948-page history of the 1789 Revolution, Schama noted that "historians have been overconfident about the wisdom to be gained by distance, believing it somehow confers objectivity, one of those unattainable values in which they have placed so much faith."[4]

Instead of distance and unattainable objectivity, therefore, Schama opted for proximity, providing the reader with probable, imagined, and hypothetical conversations between various participants of the Revolution, invented descriptions of their dress, emotions, and reactions to political events and even to the weather. He chose, in other words, to present his "arguments in the form of a narrative," a form of discourse that, as he defiantly noted, is "a fictional device used by historians to impose a reassuring order on randomly arriving bits of information about the dead."[5]

The historical record on its own, it seems, was simply a meaningless chronological record until fleshed out and re-composed into something intelligible. The Italian author Luigi Pirandello made the same point when he observed that real historical life is often so filled with the absurd, the fantastic, and the coincidental that only those who have lived through it could believe it. Were such things to be put into fiction, no one would believe them. "Life's absurdities don't have to seem believable, because they are real. As opposed to art's absurdities which, to seem real, have to be believable."[6] Art, in short, has a much easier time of it, for it need only compose something believable. A historian has to take real coincidences and strange events and make them believable. Turning history—randomly arriving names, dates, battles, and so on—into something that makes sense, however, means turning the data into a story, a task that requires imagination, narrative ability, and poetic license.

To use poetic composition to make a meaningful point is hardly new. In ancient times, primitive peoples often turned natural events such as thunder, the stars, or the rustle of leaves into divine messages and composed human actions into superhuman legends to make their heroes memorable. Such imaginative and creative interpretations of reality helped early people interpret the world and its gods and demons just as our social thinkers compose events in a rational manner so we can understand them. Many important thinkers[7] have argued that poetic interpretation was as natural to early humanity as our scientific and philosophical explanation is to us. Poetry here, of course, does not mean "expression in verse," but the imaginative composition of the world in ways that seem to make it intelligible or meaningful.

This early poetic interpretation of reality is especially interesting because of its religious and moral or ethical dimensions. In the earliest times, order and morality did not exist. Everything had to be invented from human ingenuity and imagination. As Vico explained it, men first created the gods and then the laws of gods. And then, believing the laws divine, men obeyed them and became moral and "civilized."[8] Though certainly bloody and cruel, the rituals and morals of people such as the Druids are immensely important because they demonstrate the way imaginative invention carved up a seamless and incoherent world and invented heaven and earth, good and evil, and relevant and irrelevant.

These fathers of human morality were not rational philosophers, but what Machiavelli called "armed prophets," rough and bloody men such as Romulus, Numa Pompilius, Cyrus, Theseus, and Moses, men who imposed their sectarian orders by the violent measures dictated by the times and their gods. Thus, poetry is associated with the founding of a people's "common sense," or what Francesco De Sanctis called "culture": "What does culture mean in this case? It means undoubtedly a coherent, unitary . . . 'conception of life and of man' . . . a philosophy that has become precisely 'a culture,' that is, it has generated an ethic, a mode of living, a civil and individual conduct."[9]

Individual poet-founders and heroic ancestors were often memorialized and their exploits magnified in epic poetry such as the *Iliad* and *Odyssey*, the *Aeneid*, the *Exodus*, *Le Chanson de Roland*, or the *Niebelungenlied*. What is important, however, is not the verse and meter of such epics—qualities that only made the moral codes and heroic exploits easier to remember—but the fact that this poetry came to be the identifying mark of particular, ethnic peoples. It was the religious and moral spirit of a people in speech, their "common sense," the thing that distinguished them from other peoples. Vico, in fact, suggested that there had never been an actual Homer, the *Iliad* and *Odyssey* being simply the spirit of the ancient Greeks composed into verse over centuries of time.[10]

In short, imaginative religious poetry percolated through every dimension of life so that nearly all of a people's speech and thought—its legal, social, and political life as well as its ordinary speech—were coterminous with religion and poetry.[11] Indeed, communal life, law, custom, and morals all seem to have had poetic and religious origins, developing from and around devotional chants, ceremonies, and supplications that were poetic in nature.[12] Such moral rules and rituals became not only the way one people distinguished itself from another, but the unifying standard that held people together as they fought their way into the future. Thus, we find Athens still permeated by the code of Homer at the time of Socrates and the Judeo-Christian world of today still reflecting the words of Moses.

ANCIENT VIEWS OF HISTORY

It is evident that early poetic society had little grasp of critical history as we know it. They took their legends and myths at face value and had little interest in finding out whether the tales of heroism and virtue had any evidence to support them. In fact, early peoples—and even people in the preindustrial West—not only had little understanding of critical history, they did not think of history as something "past." And having had no industrial revolution or "technological breakthroughs," they had good reason to believe that little had changed in the thousands of years that humans had been on earth. The "advance" of history that we regard as normal was simply unknown. Moral codes and other ideas never became outdated or lost their relevance.

Even in the late medieval world, which believed the calendar had begun with the birth of Christ—and might, therefore, have conceptualized a *developing* history—there was no interest in the subject. Indeed, history had no place in the university curriculum in either the *trivium* or the *quadrivium.*[13] History was simply the sorry story of man's journey on earth, the prelude to one's real life, which began after death. As late as the seventeenth century, it was normal to think that Roman and Greek statesmen, heroes, and founders lived just as later people did, made love and war as they did, and so were fit models for all times. The tales of the past were thus not subjected to "critical history," but treated as examples of moral exhortation, source books of heroic virtues to be emulated in order to make good citizens who would maintain the natural and eternal order.[14] The Greeks, like the Romans, thus treated historical legend as a poem, an exhortation to duty.[15] In effect, well into modern times, people lived without history, in an order of things that seemed never to change.

To write a scientific "history"—that is, historiography as we know it—of an eternal order would have been as meaningless as writing a history of the seasons, the monotonous cycle of the birth and death of humans, animals, plants, and cities which, if noticed at all, "occasioned world-weariness and *angst*."[16] To ask what such history "meant" or what it was going "to do" was meaningless. Poetic history, on the other hand, provided models for living in this eternal world. It taught one "the eternal hierarchies of unchanging nature . . . [and the] immemorial continuities of traditional behavior."[17]

The Ancient Quarrel between Philosophy and Poetry

Since the eighteenth century, philosophers, scientists, and historians have come to believe that poetry and myth can and should be overcome by critical reason. "How, indeed," asked Gibbon in the enlightened eighteenth century, "was it possible that a philosopher should accept as divine truths the idle tales of the poets, and the incoherent traditions of antiquity?"[18]

This dispute between local poetic thought, idle tales, and traditions on the one hand and universal and eternal reason on the other is, however, an old quarrel. Overcoming the tradition of Homeric poetry with reason was one of the major ambitions of Classical Greek philosophy; but the conflict seems to have been age-old even then. In *The Republic*, Plato remarked that "there is an *old* quarrel between philosophy and poetry."[19] Plato's ideas about how or even if reason or philosophy could cut through historical tradition and legend to reality are complex and elusive; but his love of philosophy and his scolding of the ancient poets for their imaginative fantasies, their crude portrayal of the immoral behavior of the gods, and especially his rejection of blind obedience to Homeric codes of morality, are well known.

Escaping the cave of imaginative fancy, however, was never easy. Even when early historians tried to rise above legend and "idle tales" and write a history of quite recent events, they believed it necessary to make the history edifying, filling in blanks in the record with imagined episodes and speeches and arranging matters so that the past reinforced what was acceptable in the present. Thus, though Thucydides claimed that his history of the Peloponnesian Wars "proceeded upon the clearest data, and . . . arrived at conclusions as exact as can be expected in [such] matters,"[20] he also sometimes invented speeches that would "make the speakers say what was in my opinion demanded of them by the various occasions, of course adhering as closely as possible to the general sense of what they really said."[21] Such an intervention in the record was not regarded as contradictory because the purpose of history was not to recount the past, but to provide uplifting examples of how to live in an unchanging world, where one was quite likely to face "the various occasions" encountered by the actors in the history. If the actual record did not provide such responses, if it was incomplete or silent, it simply needed to be embellished and recomposed in order to provide the proper lesson. Thucydides, in short, made his speakers into poetic types, universals to illustrate the points he wanted to make.

Aristotle was even less interested in scientific history. If poetry was lower than rational thought, he said, then factual history was even lower, *beneath* poetry. Poetry and art could be useful, he allowed, but only as subordinate allies of philosophy, that is, only if they shaped and composed the past to illustrate rational philosophical truths and universals. An empirical history, however, was a useless recapitulation of the record that taught nothing; for it merely recounted what happened on a particular day to a particular individual.[22] What could be instructive about that? Thus, if history was to be anything at all, it had to rise to poetic configuration and support theory or philosophy.

The shifting of the foundation of society from poetic historical legend to reason constituted nothing less than an epistemological revolution, a redefinition of thought that excluded imagination and poetic vision and included only rational truth about the natural order. Thus, poetry, once the first form of knowledge, the source of morals and civil order, now became an inferior form of "knowledge," one that composed things in pretty verses and imaginative and figurative tropes.[23] It could be useful as the handmaiden of rational thought, but in an ideal world one would not need such stuff because truth could be stated clearly and distinctly, without resort to metaphor and myth. Poetic speech is, therefore, often seen by philosophers as related to rhetoric, a suspicious form of speech that plays upon imagination and that deceives or hides the truth.

On the other hand, of course, for those schooled in the ideas and morals of the poets—in Homeric ideas of virtue or the Pentateuch of Moses, for example—it was the *philosopher*'s attempt to find a "rational" morality that was deceptive. Claiming that the world was rational, the philosophers argued that only by casting aside the visions of the primal poets could the true nature of the world of men and things be grasped. It should, therefore, be no surprise that Homeric Athenians put Socrates to death for "corrupting the youth." Nor for that matter should it be surprising that in times when philosophy and reason had the upper hand men such as Isocrates, Cicero, Vico, and Machiavelli, who insisted on the irrational nature of the world, should have fared so poorly.[24] Likewise, today, the heirs of the Greek philosophers who maintain that factual histories are superior to legend and poetry accuse Schama and figures such as "Hayden White and the journal *History and Theory* . . . [who insist on] the fictional character of historical narrative" of putting "the discipline of history at risk."[25] They too, it seems, "corrupt the youth." In short, the "old quarrel" is still unresolved.

It is difficult for moderns today to understand how anyone could have maintained that the unity of poetry, rhetoric, common sense, and ordinary speech could have any relationship to truth. We, the participants, or at least the heirs of the "modern project" insist that all of our beliefs should derive from or be grounded in the much higher standard of critical reason and scientific truth. We are, in this sense, heirs of Plato and Aristotle, of the idea that reason is superior to legend as philosophy is to poetry.

THE MODERN PROJECT

Thinkers today dispute the origin of the modern belief that the world is rational and that logical reason and speech must be grounded in that rational order. Some, like Martin Heidegger and Jacques Derrida, for example, argue that "modernity" had been "destined" ever since philosophers such as Plato, Aristotle, and earlier figures like Parmenides[26] proposed the idea that nature and humanity shared a common, rational language whose supremacy could only be ensured by having reason vanquish imagination. Others see the beginning of the modern era much later, in the Renaissance, that "re-birth" of the West after the long night of the Christian Dark Ages.[27] Still others, perhaps most, argue that modernity really only began with the scientific revolution of the seventeenth century, with the thought of Galileo, Descartes, and the *philosophes* of the later Enlightenment[28] who believed that they had found in analytic geometry and the calculus a common language with nature.[29]

Whenever modernity began, however, its underlying conviction was that since everything operated according to rational laws and not by fate or chance, *everything*—even history—could and eventually would be known.[30] The knowledge that resulted from this "modern project" would not, moderns believed, be confined to nature but would even include social and human things; and it is here that the modern scientific spirit competed most fiercely with earlier poetry and revealed religion. Both perspectives claimed to provide a total explanation of the human condition. Religion provided closure through faith, the belief that although inexplicable events had explanations, that the absurd trials of Job had meaning, mere human reason could never access God's mysterious ways. Religion, in other words, assured its adherents that the world had a logos; but religion accepted the limits of human reason and the existence of miracle and mystery. Reason also, however, provided a total explanation through faith, in this case, the faith that mere human reason could eliminate inexplicable phenomena altogether. Human reason did not, in other words, eliminate the omnipotent God; it absorbed Him. Science *became* God, omniscient and potentially, therefore, omnipotent. Despite science's ridicule of religion, therefoe, there was a kind of religious aura or mystique to science.[31]

To eliminate mystery and chance meant that there must be discoverable natural laws for civilization that could command assent the same way that the laws of gravity did. Evidently, myth and the persistence of tradition obscured these laws; and the way to make them clear was "simply" to eradicate poetic myth and other traditional legends. The great advantage of rational laws was not only that they would be self-evident but that they would be universal and would, therefore, supersede the mere sectarian prejudices of the ancient poets, religious leaders, and uneducated traditionalists. With truth understood in universal terms, no one could defend iniquity. Violence would recede with the advance of knowledge and the elimination of the traditions of particular societies. Philosophy, therefore, had a revolutionary mission. It was to begin the world over again, providing it with a natural and rational foundations. The genealogical line from this belief forward to the French Revolutionaries and their radical attempt to begin the world over again, their extraordinary declaration that 1792 was now "the year I," is clear.

Until the seventeenth century, the general belief in an eternal unchanging world had made historical leaps inconceivable. Indeed, the idea of historical progress or development would have threatened history's poetic value in conveying moral virtue; for if the world was developing, the moral virtues of the past were no longer relevant. The eighteenth-century belief that history could be overcome, that one could discard it by leaping into the uncluttered state of nature, therefore, constituted a momentous change. Moderns, with their logical and mathematical reason and their Newtonian physics, had crossed a threshold that seemed to make earlier thinking superfluous. Thus, in the seventeenth and eighteenth centuries it became possible to regard history as the foolishness of the past.

Though nineteenth-century thinkers continued the modern project, never doubting its fundamental tenet that the world had rational, orderly, and discoverable principles, they were not as contemptuous of the past as many Enlightenment thinkers had been. Indeed, in the nineteenth century history emerged as a kind of master discipline. This new respect for history led in two general directions. One school of thought determined to found a science of history. Instead of dismissing history as the foolishness of the past, in other words, these intellectuals wanted to study it with the same methods that natural scientists studied nature. Objectivity, careful scrutiny of the historical fact, and unbiased reflection, they reasoned, could yield an objective and universal history of humanity from its origin to the present. Such a scientific history, laying fact upon fact and statistic upon statistic, might be time-consuming, but once complete, it would be a universal reference work, as sound an empirical record as any descriptive science could be. As the nineteenth-century historian Henry Thomas Buckle (1821–1862) put it, "Those who have a steady conception of the regularity of events, and have firmly seized the great truth that the actions of men . . . are in reality never inconsistent, but . . . only form part of one vast scheme of universal order . . . . [will see that] the progress of inquiry is becoming so rapid and so earnest, that [there can be] little doubt that before another century has elapsed, the chain of evidence will be complete."[32]

Like Buckle, the German historian, Leopold von Ranke (1795–1886), the so-called Nestor of historians because of his importance in founding modern historical methods, sought to make history a science, a morally neutral record of the facts. Thus, in introducing his famous *Histories of the Latin and Germanic Nations*, he noted that at one time "history ha[d] been assigned the office of judging the past, of instructing the present for the benefit of future ages. To such high offices *this work does not aspire*: It wants only to show what actually happened (*wie es eigentlich gewesen*)."[33] For Ranke, such a history would eventually comprise a "universal history, from the beginning to the present day. Universal history comprehends the past life of mankind, not in its particular relations and trends, but in its fullness and totality. . . . The final goal—not yet attained—always remains the conception and the composition of a history of mankind."[34] It was a tall order; for even recording what a particular individual did in a single day, let alone "mankind" in all its history, could fill a volume.[35]

Against this idea that history was a merely descriptive science that had "nothing to teach," there developed the competing idea that history had "everything" to teach. This school held that a careful scrutiny of the past revealed something much more important than an objective record. Indeed, it revealed that history had a life and a purpose of its own in which individual humans were secondary. Humans were passengers on a journey in which they could participate, but not alter. In short, to these thinkers, the study of history revealed a *philosophy* of history, an understanding of where history was taking humanity. There certainly were, in other words, rational principles in the world. They were not to be found in nature, however, but in the course of history. History, therefore, was not the erroneous beliefs and practices of an ignorant past, but the development of a rational World Spirit that had ends greater than the self-interested and lesser ends of individual men. In short, humans might not be rational; but history was. As Hegel famously put it, "The sole thought which philosophy brings to the treatment of history is the simple concept of *Reason*: that Reason is the law of the world and that, therefore, in world history, things have come about rationally."[36]

This subordination of all world history to a theory, to the idea that the philosopher could step out of history and understand where it was going, must rank as one of the greatest, if most dubious and self-congratulatory, beliefs of modernity. To Hegelians and later Marxists, the forward direction that history had chosen was clear.[37] The industrial revolution, the French Revolution, expanding democracy, and material plenty seemed to indicate that whatever trials humans had to bear were the cost of history's determination to reach a final rational society. Everything that had happened did so for a reason. It might be maddeningly slow, but history knew where it was going and was going there as fast as it could go.[38]

Society, in other words, could not leapfrog over the horrible stages of history to the final rational order as the *philosophes* and the French revolutionaries had wanted to do any more than an individual could leap straight from infancy into middle-aged maturity. Thinkers such as Hegel and Marx and popularizers of Darwin began to see history, therefore, not as Gibbon's "register of the crimes, follies, and misfortunes of mankind,"[39] but as the vehicle that would conduct humanity to some kind of resolution. It was a long dialectical journey, but as one error after another proved a blind alley, humanity's woes would decrease over time, and the path to reason and tranquility would steadily narrow.[40] History, in short, had a life of its own; and humans were free to participate in it or else get run over by it. Hegelian dialectical reason, Marxist class warfare, and Darwinian "survival of the fittest" were all metaphors for this historical engine of progress.

This theory of a philosophy of history constituted, like the earlier subordination of poetry to philosophy, a momentous metaphysical revolution and in many respects the capstone of the great "modern project," the pursuit of the *logos* or ultimate rationality of things. In short, when historians influenced by Hegelian or Marxist thought said they could know history, they did not mean simply knowing some string of data within history, like the presidents of the United States. They meant that they understood that the *purpose* of the historical engine was resolution of conflict through the complete knowledge of nature, human consciousness, or the achievement of a classless society. It might be far off, but it was inevitable.[41]

Whether one followed the scientific historians like Ranke and his heirs or the philosophical historians such as Hegel and Marx and their heirs, there was a supreme confidence among historians that human history could at last be known, that the record of cause and effect, the string of data, could be traced back to its origin and forward to the present. Scientific historians might concentrate on more empirical projects—the origins of the French Revolution or the Great War—and philosophical historians on the meaning of it all, but they held in common the idea that events did not happen accidentally or by coincidence or miracle. History had discoverable and demonstrable causes and, therefore, everything could be and would be known. Accidents, of course, did happen; and chance events occurred. But they were not "world historical" and could not derail the inexorable rational and/or structural forces that moved beneath the surface phenomena. This belief that mere humans could know everything, so remarkably different from an age that still knew Prometheus, Pandora, and Adam united both philosophical and scientific historians in a common conviction: History seemed headed to some kind of extraordinary resolution. The great questions, the interminable class conflicts, the frightening reign of mystery and chance all seemed about end.

The essence of this self-confident demeanor was not confined to the study of history. It percolated through all forms of knowledge; and is captured in the cheery swagger of the Nobel prize-winning physicist Max Born, who having just become acquainted with Paul Dirac's equations for the electron, boasted to some visitors at Gottigen University back in 1928 that "physics, as we know it, will be over in six months."[42] In other words, there was a unity in modern cosmology, a belief that everything would fall into place as an all-embracing system that left behind no puzzles: "The idea guiding our meditations," wrote the philosopher of phenomenology, Edmund Husserl, in 1929, "[is] the Cartesian idea of a science that shall be established as radically genuine, ultimately an all-embracing science."[43]

The belief in rational understanding conveyed through rational language and deployed against imagination, myth, and poetry is the heritage into which many of us were born, or as Heidegger says, into which we were "thrown." It is still the governing assumption of many thinkers that humanity, collectively and individually, is engaged in a struggle to rid the world of poetic myths and to ground it in rational understanding and truth.

THE CRISIS OF MODERNITY

Deciding to engage in the struggle to defeat poetry and myth and establish or demonstrate the existence of a rational order rests, of course, on the assumption that there *is* such a thing as the truth and a rational outcome. Suppose, however, truth is merely a human construct. Then rational thought too, would be a poem, an epic about a hero, Reason. Of course, reason might still defeat all other forms of thought; but we might be a little suspicious over having to submit to the dream of a mere human hero. We might wonder whether the rule of this hero, with its imperious ability to eliminate poetry, religion, chance, and "mistaken" choice, would be desirable. It is the suspicion that the rational order is such a dream, and one that just might come true, that now haunts contemporary thought.

No one knows why or how great grounding assumptions such as the belief in objective truth or progress lose their credibility;[44] but when belief systems of such magnitude give out, common sense itself seems to be evaporating. Such crises were not unknown in the past. Classical Greece and the seventeenth century Baroque era, for example, were periods of such *Angst*. The reaction of the Athenians to Socrates' interminable questions was a rather tepid response from a society in such circumstances. More dramatic are the sixteenth and seventeenth-century horrors that followed the breakup of the *respublica Christiana*, the appearance of the various protestant sects, and the arrival of a secular philosophy that challenged *all* religion. "New philosophy," lamented the Baroque poet John Donne (1572–1631), "calls all in doubt. . . . . 'Tis all in peeces, all cohaerence gone." Like Donne, many today feel that modernity's common sense is "all in peeces." The belief that we were slowly but surely closing in on truth and plenty, that evolution had ended—as God intended—with humanity,[45] has suddenly begun to ring hollow. We are no longer sure that the engine of progress exists or if it exists, that it is taking us where we want to go.

One way to conceive this "crisis of modernity" is to suggest that the modern social and physical scientists occupied for moderns the same position that the poets held centuries ago for prescientific peoples. In other words, as earlier peoples accepted the moral and physical world given them by their poets, so moderns understood that same world as their physical and social scientists interpreted it to them. And just as the moral concepts and practices anchored to ancient myths were shaken and then gave way, so now modern moral concepts and practices seem to be giving way to the suspicion that the ideas of modernity's social and physical scientists might also be poetic tales. This so-called "crisis of modernity" and the birth of postmodern thought is the atmosphere of contemporary life.

What made moderns, with their science, their confidence, and their reason, lose their belief is not clear. Perhaps it was the millions and millions of deaths in modern wars, the staggering tens of millions of deaths "history" required to build Stalin's Russia or Mao's China,[46] or perhaps the vanquishing of modern armies in Vietnam and Afghanistan by premodern fighters, or simply the blatant insignificance of individual life in the immense, bureaucratized, rational, streamlined, and efficient world that reason seems to have created. Whatever the cause, confidence in history and in the advance of modernity in the late twentieth century seems to have ended in a kind of metaphysical flame-out.

This fear and pessimism is not just continental; it haunts the West as a whole. At any rate, it haunts its intellectuals and seems to underlie acres of recent texts on contemporary social theory. Alasdair MacIntyre, for example, begins his significantly titled *After Virtue* by noting that "we are all already in a state so disastrous that there are no large remedies for it." To Robert Bellah, whose research team investigated middle-class America in 1985, it seems that we are "hovering on the very brink of disaster, not only from international conflict but from the internal incoherence of our own society. What," he cried, "has gone wrong? How can we reverse the slide toward the abyss?" Likewise, Robert Heilbroner, in October 1991, noted the appearance of "a silent depression," a horrific "economic decline." "At the apparent zenith of its triumph, its enemies confounded, America seems headed for disaster. What may seem a hyperbole is only to repeat what I hear on every side. The country is visibly decaying. I do not know anyone who sees a bright future for it."

One of the most surprising things about this all-pervasive gloom is that it stretches across the political spectrum from left to right. Cornel West, author of *Race Matters* (1993)[47] and one of the editors of a widely-read 1985 series of essays on postmodern or postanalytical thought, is convinced that "we live among the ruins of North Atlantic civilization. . . . . As we approach the end of the twentieth century, the rich intellectual resources of the West are in disarray and a frightening future awaits us." And from the other end of the spectrum, Leo Strauss, one of the most profound and influential conservative thinkers of our era, predicted that modern thought would lead Western civilization into a new Dark Age: "One may say of [contemporary political science] that it fiddles while Rome burns. It is excused by two facts: it does not know that it fiddles, and it does not know that Rome burns."

Certainly one of the most apocalyptic visions of the contemporary world runs through Francis Fukuyama's widely read *The End of History and the Last Man*. According to Fukuyama, the whole idea of faith in a rational history had been mistaken. It was not that reason would be *defeated* that bothers Fukuyama; but that it would win. The last phase of history, says Fukuyama, will certainly be rational. But it will be the end of the human *spirit*, the reign of Nietzsche's "last men." The "last men" represent the happiness and *Sitzfleisch* that always brings up the rear in the retreat of civilization, the lethargic human cockroaches that can adapt to anything because they believe in nothing. Unlike moderns who saw the last men as the beneficiaries of the long march of history to reason and democracy, Fukuyama finds that "the last man's situation [will be] worse as a result of the entire historical process . . . [that led] human society toward democracy." Unlike moderns who wanted to hurry history along, Fukuyama finds that "the soberest and most thoughtful minds of this century have seen no reason to think that the world is moving toward what we in the West consider decent and human political institutions. . . . The future is more likely than not to contain new and unimagined evils, from fanatical dictatorships and bloody genocides to the banalization of life through modern consumerism . . . unprecedented disasters awaits us from nuclear winter to global warming."

Setting the tone for all these gloomy accounts, and casting his shadow over the whole postmodern era is, of course, the ghost of Martin Heidegger, who in his sermon of 1947, announced ominously that "only a God can save us." And acceptance of Heidegger's message has become a kind of condition of the possibility of being taken seriously as a postmodern intellectual.[48]

"Postmodernity" is a term that requires definition. In a now famous essay first published in 1979, Jean-Francois Lyotard gave the classic definition of postmodernism: "incredulity toward metanarratives."[49] A metanarrative is the mental framework or paradigm in which thought operates. It is, in other words, essential to thought itself. Without such a paradigm, thought would be utterly open-ended and faced with a terrifying and infinite possibility. Life without a metanarrative would be like being transported to another universe where literally everything would have to be learned from experience. Everything would be new; and anything could do anything. In short, common sense would evaporate.[50]

The word *metanarrative* derives from a much earlier term, *metaphysics*, which meant knowledge of the whole, of things physical and beyond. Metaphysics, like the metanarrative, walls off the terrifying world where anything can do anything. By experience, logic, imagination, or divination, metaphysics builds categories where things behave themselves. Aristotle, for example, set the parameters of inquiry for centuries with the metaphysic of teleology, the assertion or assumption that the human and natural worlds had a natural "end" or "purpose" (a *telos*) and that human and physical things moved naturally ("teleologically") toward their "telos."

One is, at first, tempted to think that other powerful ideas such as "progress," "Divine law," "natural law," "survival of the fittest," and so on are also examples of metanarratives. And, in a way, they are. But all of them, and teleology as well, are metaphors for a still greater metanarrative, namely the belief that there *is* a discoverable, rational order to history, the universe, and eventually, for human society.

The suspicion that there is no such *logos*, that human reason is a mere artificial filter imposed on a fundamentally "irrational" world is what characterizes postmodernity. The idea is staggering because, if it is correct, the entire Western world has been on a false scent since the time of the Greeks. In other words, if this "rational assumption" is but a myth, a twenty-five-hundred year old "whistle-in-the-dark," how distant is the belief in the *logos* from the prayers of primitive peoples who hoped that the pandemonium they saw about them was only appearance, the facade that hid the order the gods must have decreed?

Lyotard's use of the word "narrative," of course, indicates his belief that the assumption about a rational order is indeed merely a fictional or poetic myth. He is not alone in this suspicion. Other postmoderns have adopted different terms than Lyotard;[51] but they all share the idea that the rational order is as grand a poem as that of Homer.

When such a vision takes hold, the loss of confidence is hard to contain. It is not surprising that it is found even in natural science. The modern view of science was generally reductionist, that is it held that all phenomena, including human consciousness, derived from certain fundamental and related mathematical equations or principles. Nothing, in other words, not God, man, or the tornado, operates according to its own autonomous principles. Such a belief has been the major ingredient of physics—and all rational thought—for a long time, back perhaps to Thales who held that everything was composed of water. Understand everything about water, in other words, and everything else—*The Whole Shebang*, as Timothy Ferris put it[52]—follows.

A century ago, few took Nietzsche seriously when he asserted that belief in a fundamental order simply tells us about the way these believers think—or hope. Today, anti-reductionism haunts scientific thought.[53] Perhaps the most famous recent assertion that belief in science might simply be a rational poem or "metanarrative" was that of the historian of science, Thomas Kuhn. In 1962, he published an unnerving and controversial book called *The Structure of Scientific Revolutions* in which he argued that the rational order was a mere "paradigm," a kind of arbitrary lens for sorting orderly things out of nature, on the assumption that, being orderly, they must be meaningful. But, Kuhn suggested, that paradigm may not be grounded in anything other than our *desire* for order, or perhaps in the fact that it is a lot easier to locate things that repeat themselves than it is to find a singularity. The paradigm, in other words, certainly finds orderly behavior; but then, that is all it is looking for.

In other words, a scientist learns by studying and following what other scientists do. He or she formulates research projects and hypotheses within that paradigm and then tests them in the world. The paradigm, in other words, *governs* or prefigures what the scientist looks for and necessarily filters out anything "irrelevant." As Kuhn points out, Aristotle and Ptolemy found perfectly satisfactory answers to their questions; even the mathematics worked. It is just that their reference frame prefigured different questions than ours.[54] It was a problem long ago pointed out by Kant: "Reason has insight only into that which it produces after a plan of its own . . . constraining nature to give answer to questions of reason's own determining."[55] In short, reason can only find what it is looking for; it may, however, not be what really matters. Kuhn later backed away from some of the more radical implications of his assertions,[56] but the idea of being confined to the paradigm of reason has reverberated through the scientific community, attracting the attention of a number of prominent scholars of the "hard" sciences.[57]

Despite the wide number of areas they treat, what these scholars have in common is a fascination with disorder and the recognition that it is everywhere and much more common than moderns thought. What interests many anti-reductionist physicists today is not only the power of random chaotic events that the rational filter regarded as mere background noise, but the possible sovereignty such events may exercise over more occasional and isolated orderly systems.

Order, in short, may only be one part of this complex and multidimensional world. And it may not be the most important. As James Gleick noted, in physics the twentieth century "will be remembered for three things: relativity, quantum mechanics, and chaos." Each of these three theories has diminished the realm of the orderly world of Newton and Laplace. As the physicist Michael Schlesinger put it, "Relativity eliminated the Newtonian illusion of absolute space and time; quantum theory eliminated the Newtonian dream of a controllable measurement process; and chaos eliminates the Laplacian fantasy of deterministic predictability." More unnerving yet, is the fact that a good deal of science works only in the controlled conditions of the laboratory. "Chaos," on the other hand, "applies to the universe we see and touch, [to] everyday experience."[58] Chance, the demon modern science had thought it had cornered, is back.

Some "hard" science has already been softened by an appreciation of the eerie power of the chance "singularity," the one-time, random event that changes the entire course of things in ways difficult if not impossible to predict. The Harvard paleontologist, Stephen Jay Gould, for example, argues that the belief that evolution selects the "fittest" reflects a self-congratulatory assumption that we humans are the "fittest," the destined product of evolution. The real engine of evolution, he says, is chance. Thus, organisms that were lucky enough to have escaped the collision of an asteroid or some other accident were the ones that survived and continued to procreate when far fitter species perished.[59] In fact, he asserts, if we could run the tape backward and begin evolution again, there is no reason at all to suppose that the human species would evolve again.

Such a conclusion is of the utmost significance, for if a random one-time event can disrupt and re-vector the orderly world, then it follows that the orderly world is a prisoner of the disorderly; and science must admit that its knowledge is and must be limited. Man, in short, is no longer God. This means that the creed of modernity, its belief that chance was ignorance and that one day we will understand everything, is impossible to hold. It was precisely this realization that led the Nobel prize-winning physicist Ilya Prigogine to argue that we can never master or understand nature. At best, we can, like the ancient priests and oracles, only hold a "conversation" or "dialogue" with nature, asking this and that, sometimes getting clear answers, other times enigmatic or ambiguous replies, still other times stubborn silence. In short, the assumption that the human convention of logical language is also nature's language may have to be abandoned.[60]

And, of course, if we doubt the logic or reason of nature, there is every reason to doubt the rational progressive order of human history.

Problems of Writing History in a Postmodern World

A good deal of recent social theory has abandoned the modern paradigm of progress, surrendered the attempt to define historical forces, and even jettisoned the traditional study of diplomatic, governmental, and other political organizations. In place of these, the tendency is to study cultural history[61] and in particular the role of language in society. Stemming perhaps from the earlier linguistic structuralism of Ferdinand de Sausurre, Claude Levi-Strauss, and others, and reformulated by Martin Heidegger's assertion that language is "the house of Being"—that is, the "structure" that most reflects the way a culture relates itself to Being, God, the *logos*, nature, or some other totem—many social theorists and writers have turned their attention to the subtle way that language shapes and protects the cultural order. On the ground that all legitimacy claims are unverifiable, these studies often consider a culture's grounding (*Grund*) only in functional terms. That is, they focus on the *implications* for society that a particular linguistic conception of Being creates, the way that key words are deployed in concepts regarded as "self-evident." Figures such as Nietzsche and, more recently, Michel Foucault and Jacques Derrida are not interested so much in exposing the arbitrary or "groundless" nature of a culture's "House of Being" as they are in highlighting the way language disguises the abyss and enforces the invisible and visible Order of Things.[62]

Derrida, for example, often points to the hidden partiality given to one term in traditional binary language systems, such as man/woman, writing/saying, white/black, and so on. According to Derrida, one term is always "marked" and exerts a "violent hierarchy" over the "other." Thus the supposedly neutral "man" or "mankind" when used to represent all humanity can be said to subordinate women. Seemingly neutral language, therefore, seems to protect patriarchy in hidden ways. Derrrida's philosophy of "deconstruction" aims at "exploding" this kind of traditional "semantic horizon."[63]

Foucault, on the other hand, is interested in the way that knowledge (*savoir*) is deployed as power (*pouvoir*). That deployment occurs through the classification of the world into different categories—males, females, buttons, and bows, and so on. What disturbs Foucault is that while classification is necessary, it is never congruent with reality. In other words, the very foundation of knowledge, the ability to classify or distinguish one thing from another, is precarious. Indeed, it is fraught with danger not only because it separates language from reality but because the separation is unnoticed. The classification system of all the disciplines is accepted as a transparent window onto reality, normal knowledge, the stuff of common sense. Foucault certainly revives here the ancient debate about the disparity between *res* and *verba*—the fact that the word can never capture the thing[64]—but his exploration of the implications that arise from this disparity is no abstract problem of "critical thinking." It is an undermining of the foundations of knowledge, especially in the human sciences.

What happens, Foucault asks, when classification is applied to humans? Psychiatrists, sociologists, physicians, sexologists, demographers, ethnologists, and so on appear. They begin, as all science must begin, by classifying their subject matter, in this case, other humans.[65] Thus people are divided into categories such as normal, abnormal, female, male, black, wealthy, homeless, and so on. Each category is assigned appropriate characteristics and from this arbitrary "knowledge" experts testify, public policy flows, organizations are "streamlined," "modernized" and "upgraded;" and subjects soon learn to conform to their "norms." Similarly, when such "knowledge" is deployed in the workplace, employees are boxed up according to productivity, performance, and team work. When "studies show," "experts agree," and "specialists say," then, according to Foucault, "knowledge" becomes *power.*

Of course, as every administrator, manager, and superior officer will affably agree (while filling out a performance rating), such categories are not meant as a measure of *worth*. But, somehow, they are. The medians, the means, and the midpoints migrate down to the doctor's office, the administrator's desk, the counselor's couch, and the classroom as knowledge to which the subject had better conform. Even disease is regarded as a fault caused by failing to conform to health standards. In short, one is left constantly jumping through hoops to try to measure up to an abstraction that may not even exist in the real world. Benevolent constabularies of bureaucrats, hygienic police, and universities are established to enforce, pass on, update, and improve the knowledge. And soon, the citizens happily police themselves. "Knowledge," in short, is a form of power, all the more insidious because it is science, indisputable. Resistance would obviously be sick or irrational.

But classifications in the human sciences, like all knowledge, are developed within the flux of history, from which point there is no way to know how or even if the classifications apply to the real world. Thus taxonomy, the "science" of classification in biology has its *own* history, changing the measure of categories from morphological appearance to cell structure to DNA analysis. And every time the measure changes, relevant species lose their former identity or must even pull up stakes and take up residence in another place.

Foucault conducts an "archaeological" dig around the early discourse of the various human sciences, showing the way their arbitrary and problematic classifications are often rooted in chance, folklore, or thin air. Nonetheless, they have come to be incorporated into the fabric of society. Foucault stresses that he is not conducting a "history" of human sciences because traditional history begins "outside" history just as the social sciences claim to study humans from outside humanity. History classifies its material as if history were "a completed development" and the evidence were "all in." Foucault's archaeology has no such solid ground; it is, as he put it, "without constants. Nothing in man—not even his body—is sufficiently stable to serve as the basis for self-recognition or for understanding other men."[66]

The implications of Foucault's work for history are momentous; for, by inserting the historian into history and pointing out the unreliable nature of traditional historical classifications, historical explanation becomes a poetic stab in the dark at what is swirling about us. Indeed, the suspicion that the modern paradigm was a poetic vision supported by arbitrary classifications has played a major role in establishing postmodern doubts not only about the theory of progress and the desirability of the ultimate resolution of things, but about the legitimacy of any explanation of history. It is certainly not that postmoderns doubt that the French Revolution, the American Civil War, the Holocaust, or the implosion of the former Soviet Union took place. Nor is it that they deny that great historical forces blow through history. Rather, it is that they realize that the number of potential triggers for such immense events is so unfathomable that they despair of ever sorting them into classes.

Moreover, classification of historical causes is not only arbitrary, it is suspiciously self-fulfilling, always successful at finding what it is looking for: Searching for instrumental economic causes, one finds instrumental economic causes; searching for social causes, one finds those; and searching for religious, political, demographic, Freudian, architectural, or even musical causes would produce the same success. Certainly some forces exist; but how can one classify forces or causes into "economic" as opposed to "social," "demographic," or "political?" Where does one put religion or war? Is "service industry" an economic, demographic, social classification, or is it political rhetoric? Is a census "demographic" or "political?" How, even if such things could be distinguished, does one determine which is major and which minor?

And it is not only the tail-chasing and arbitrary nature of this search for the cause that interests postmoderns, it is the knowledge that the path-changing events of history may not be these forces or events at all, but simply some unexpected random event. But how could one design a filter for the unexpected? The point of a paradigm is to uncover the hidden variable and mark out its effects, steadily narrowing it down until it and its effect are expected. The truly unexpected puts in an appearance in a totally random and spontaneous fashion, from nowhere. In short, the purpose of the paradigm is to limit the search. But chance seems to be ubiquitous, exercising a terrifying suzerainty over things that happened and even those that did not: It was chance that Lenin was born; chance that he arrived safely in Russia in 1917; it was chance that Kennedy did not lean down and scratch his leg that fateful day in Dallas; chance that the plot against Hitler failed and so on. Looking for chance, in other words, is precisely what a historical explanation cannot do.

Finally, what makes traditional cause and effect explanation suspect is that the random event is frequently a human individual, the genius, the madman, or the grand strategist that turns up out of the blue and makes things veer off in a startling way. Historical explanation, however, rounds up all these "ususal suspects" and makes them accessories to deep tectonic forces such as economics or demographics that supposedly guide history. Thus, modern rational history or philosophy of history could not regard it as an "explanation" to say that the Russian revolution happened because of Lenin or that World War I occurred because of "some damn fool thing in the Balkans" as Bismarck predicted. Such a conclusion would reduce history to the individual and the accidental, for which there can be no philosophy or science.

Modern history prefers the Big Picture where Lenin's arrival in St. Petersburg was but an episode in the larger unfolding Russian revolution that was destined by economic, social, or perhaps political forces. Likewise, Francis Ferdinand's assassination was simply the "occasion" for a war that would have happened anyway, because of the collapse of the old order, economic and colonial rivalries, or some other seismic cause. In other words, historical explanation buries the random event and individual choice and convinces us that had Lenin never existed or Gavrilo Princip's bullets not found their mark, history, with a few minor changes, would have continued on its destined course anyway. In modern historical explanation then, real life is always grounded in something larger than chance and individual choice. In other words, history assumes for us the role earlier humans had assigned to an omniscient God who also forbade accidents and freak bull's-eyes.

Postmoderns, on the other hand, suspect that history would have been very different without Lenin and the assassination in Sarajevo. They also suspect that historians would have explained that very different history by making it a result of the same forces they now use to explain the history that *did* happen. Historical explanation cannot admit that things—big things, too—happen at random and by chance and individual choice. History with a big "H" always steps in and makes chance and choice only "apparent," an illusion on the surface of the seismic forces for which theory claims to have a rational explanation. For postmoderns, little history is explained by big History which is, in turn, explained by things we cannot define. They suspect, as the ancients did, that history is filled with fortune, *tyche*, and inexplicable "discontinuities" that traditional history has swept under the rug. Chance, therefore, is not a hidden variable that will restore explanation after the data is all in. Rather, it is something built into history and, therefore, constitutes for us a kind of original sin, a limit to knowledge.

This realization that knowledge is limited by an inherently flawed classification of causes and by the roles that chance and choice play in human affairs threatens the entire concept of history as we have inherited it; for without the ability to classify forces and causes, all historical explanation becomes poetic. It is not, in other words, simply that grand theories such as Hegelianism and Marxism fail because historical forces are undefinable but *all* explanations that attempt to trace the origin of an event to a cause are untenable. All, in short, rely on a one-dimensional account of a multidimensional world where risk, contingency, and the instability of the human order are excluded or downplayed.

Lacking a causal theory then, postmoderns no longer understand how to interpret things. History becomes simply the record of human reactions to events that set off various other unexpected events with which humans must cope, thereby setting off still further unexpected events. History, thus seems to be, as Henry Ford is supposed to have said, "just one damned thing after another," a discharge of meaningless flotsam and jetsam that can never be reduced to a theory.

But, because we want to believe history means something and can teach us something, we are reluctant to surrender deep explanation or to give fortune too large a place in our lives. There is something that makes one squirm when Simon Schama implies that it was chance that produced the French Revolution of 1789. Louis XVI, it happened, was just not a forceful person. Always in "a mood of nervous vacillation," he represented a contradiction in terms, a "despotism that failed to have the courage of its convictions."[67] In the orthodox reference frame, of course, the demise of the *ancien regime* was caused by deep structural forces—class conflict, the industrial revolution, the emergence of capitalism, evolving democracy—that were bigger than Louis, or anyone else for that matter. In Schama's view, however, the *ancien regime* could have been preserved by better political acumen, that is, if only Louis had had such acumen. Schama's suggestion cuts to the heart of modern historiography; for in most modern cosmology; it was *that* revolution that got progress going. Without it, the world would not have a model for leaving the feudal order in the dust, as all modern societies must. To suppose, in other words, that the revolution was merely a "French affair" that could have been avoided, in other words, is to make *THE* revolution no longer a rite of passage into modernity but bad luck, the result of a mere character flaw. This is like suggesting that had Pharaoh's daughter caught a fly in her eye that famous day in the bulrushes, the entire Judeo-Christian order would have floated on out of history. The mind resists such ideas. We do not like to think that the French Revolution occurred because Louis merely zigged when he might have zagged; or that the Judeo-Christian order came into being because a fly did not land in the eye of an Egyptian girl. But we can only avoid such ideas by claiming that "big things" such as the Russian or French Revolution or the Judeo-Christian order have metaphysical causes. They are, in other words, beyond either chance or human intervention so that individuals and their choices are no longer relevant.

The problem with this metaphysic of history, however, is not only that it eliminates the accidental and the individual, but that when such explanations of history get accepted as "knowledge," they render the real world into something too mechanical and simple. In short, the hiatus Foucault points out between word and thing separates the language of history from the historical world. Such a rupture is extremely difficult to apprehend, however, because it only appears in the past tense, when a classification scheme becomes quite obviously out of date. Thus, until the recent collapse of the Marxist intellectual hegemony, it was nearly impossible to imagine the French Revolution in terms other than class conflict. But following the crisis of Marxism in May 1968, entirely new causal factors have been elicited for the 1789 Revolution.[68] In other words, the categories always appear transparent in the present and only lose their status as self-evident knowledge after we have new categories. Common sense, it seems, evaporates the moment it becomes visible.

It is for this reason that postmodern history makes little of history's overall direction, purpose, or the metaphysical causes of change. Indeed, Foucault implies that "discontinuities" between one classificatory paradigm or *episteme,* as he calls it, occur simply because they occur; gaps between one period and another are, therefore, to be expected. This means, as it did to Nietzsche, that the appearance of potent new *epistemes* such as "rational" that legitimate and percolate through entire cultures are born by mere chance.[69] The idea of such abrupt "discontinuities," autonomous "series," and "limits," are, of course, foreign to traditional history, which tends to see a clear line back from the present time to the "Origin." There are no such assurances in Foucault. Ideas, important ideas loaded with implications, appear and disappear like comets. Though there are certainly differences and disagreements among postmodern scholars, there seems to be a new appreciation of chance and mystery, a recognition of the limits of knowledge, and a general suspicion of ever grasping the engine of "history."

Many, however, feel that the evaporation of the metaphysic of progress and the subversion of causal explanation have left us in an abyss. In other words, while deep historical analysis may have deprived us of our freedom and individuality, the "deconstruction" of modernity seems to imply a world where no classification at all can be accepted as natural, as "unconstructed." Certainly some postmodern literature is hyperbolic and charged; but postmodern theory also allows us to glimpse not only the precarious nature of classification and, therefore, of knowledge, but a more realistic picture of the place of the individual in history. Certainly the role of that individual is circumscribed by the nature of historical forces that we do not understand and by the fact that since we cannot isolate causes, we can never be sure of what effects our actions will produce. Humans in history set off unexpected cascades of events when they do anything: Invent a fixed-wing aircraft and all modern warfare changes; solve the problem of disease and create the population bomb. We are, in short, in a conversation with history, as Prigogine suggested we were with nature. Still, limited freedom is more freedom than the man-eating machine modern history created. Whether human action is free or determined is, of course, an age-old and probably irresolvable question. But whatever freedom humans *do* have can only grasped by realizing that theories of history and causal explanations that denied freedom were merely poetic metaphors for what we do not understand.

TOWARD A NEW POETIC HISTORY

Writing histories that beg the question of the cause of change and leave humans inside history, however, makes many fear that without this center of gravity, research will simply degenerate, as one of the most gifted historians of our time worried, into a jumble of kaleidoscopic snapshots, an "unending pursuit of new topics."[70] Such a degeneration is possible. But abandoning structural history may instead focus research where it is most needed.

Benedetto Croce, for example, observed that all serious history is inspired by the desire to solve some contemporary problem. Historical knowledge is an "act of comprehending and understanding induced by the requirements of practical life." Resolving contemporary practical needs "is at the bottom of every historical judgement and confers upon every history the character of contemporary history. Even though the facts that pertain may seem chronologically distant or very remote, in reality history always refers to the needs of the present situation." For history to be inspired by "practical life" certainly implies that the focus will change as present needs change; but this is as it should be for "every serious historiography and every serious philosophy ought to be a historiography and a philosophy 'for the occasion'. . . . The occasion . . . of history [lies] in the conduct of [contemporary] life and morality."[71] In other words, making historical inquiry flow from the needs of practical life in the present, far from leading to an unfocused, "unending pursuit of new topics," seems to constitute a limit; it mandates that history address the present concerns of the culture.

The problem here, however, is that until now we believed that history contained the answer to the present problem, that is, its cause. We need instead to remember that "cause" is indeterminable. This is not only because of the limits of classification and the paradigm, but because with most problems any attempt to look to history for the cause reveals that those with one view of the present problem will find one past, those with another, a still different past. Arabs and Israelis, like Protestants and Catholics in Northern Ireland, and proponents and opponents of privatization of Social Security do not agree on the historical cause of the contemporary problem any more than opponents and supporters of the Vietnam war agree on its origin or politically left and right historians in America could agree on the causes of the 1960s. The reason, obviously, is that we believe that finding the cause of the problem prescribes the remedy—who is at fault and who must pay. In other words, because history arises out of a contemporary problem, it cannot allow the past to rest in peace.

In short, establishing a historical cause for the problem constitutes a form of political argument for the present. It is to deploy power in the form of historical knowledge; and the key to success in the present is to have one's version of the past accepted as "knowledge" in Foucault's sense. The reason history is important, then, is not to find out why something really happened, something we could not know even if politics were not an issue, but that different peoples believe it happened in a certain way or want others to believe that it happened that way. History, therefore, helps to define a person or a people's position in the historical flux and to argue their political point of view.

Once we understand that "cause" is a political statement designed to help us shape our perspective on the present, we can see that historical cause is not an innocuous word, but one of those classificatory terms that is laden with power, that shapes and protects or undermines and subverts an order of things. This inherent power of history, moreover, cannot be eliminated by appeals to an outside historian "arbitrator" devoted to the truth, because it is impossible to be outside history; and it is beyond human capacity to design a taxonomy that will sort "real" cause from non-cause. In any case, no one would willingly sacrifice their vision of the cause of the problem to an outsider who does not have to live with the consequences of so-called impartial truth.

To say that historical argument is political argument is not to reduce or demean history; but to ennoble it, to rescue it from passive memorization and make the past part of the active debate. Arguing about the past, defining and defending *our* past, is a valuable and necessary part of defining ourselves in the present. It is, therefore, critical that no one else gain the power to relate another's past. Just as an individual would feel violated or want to make changes in a biographer's narrative of his or her life, so a people whose history is told by others have lost their autonomy, their right to say who they are, and are violated. There can, therefore, be no universal history, no objective history, that does not subordinate particular histories to an arbitrary imposition. Such an Orwellian nightmare can only be avoided by abandoning the universal perspective and defending the writing of history that supports what is good for one's self, one's group, or one's country. History, in short, is very serious business.

This is not to reduce history to partisan cheerleading; but to recognize that it is political. And the political is never univocal but always equivocal; it is necessarily a process of deliberation and debate that should not be suppressed by "truth." The hypothetical "universal view" or the views of others are useful as correctives, of course, as a check on self-righteousness and hubris. This should not, however, extend to a surrender of one's own views or to "sociology of values"and relativist detachment, for this implies that no history is worth defending too seriously.

Detachment has a lot of support from those who believe that evil derives from having a point of view or that concern with one's own rather the Other is itself immoral. In other words, if everyone tolerated everything, nothing could cause violence to erupt. There are at least two reasons to oppose such a perspective. The first is that tolerating everything means defending nothing. Or, put differently, until iniquity disappears in the Other, resisting evil seems to be the only way to prevent its victory. Secondly, the belief that scientific inquiry into anything, let alone social and political issues, is really neutral strains credibility. Even Ranke, who claimed that history was pure "value-free" science, was convinced that when the "evidence was all in" and the universal science complete, it would put his own country in its proper place, at the lead, for though "the knowledge of the history of mankind should be a common property of humanity [it] should above all benefit our own nation, without which our work could not have been accomplished."[72] A century later one can be even more dubious about the universal; for the work of Heidegger, Derrida, Foucault, and others, to say nothing of the contemporary literature of political correctness, has shown that bias and a political point of view can be found everywhere and especially in the self-evident.

To abandon the determination to defend one's own history and to surrender to the "universal" is to forget that flattening a complex and multidimensional history into Truth (orthodoxy, "knowledge") inevitably subordinates some to others. In short, the desire for truth is so powerful a compulsion that one must exert every energy to resist it; for no one ever knows when one will become its victim. As Foucault put it, "Truth isn't outside power or lacking in power . . . truth isn't the reward of free spirits. . . . Truth is a thing of this world: it is produced only by virtue of multiple forms of constraint. And it induces regular effects of power. Each society has its regime of truth, its 'general politics' of truth: that is, the types of discourse which it accepts and makes function as true and false statements." The only way that history can be rescued from "knowledge" or "truth" is to recognize it as political argument, a politicization of the past that is for some reason usually disparaged. Raising truth over the political is possible only for those who believe they have the truth and that everyone must hear and submit to it. "Good heavens!" said Socrates to Euthyphro, "most men would not know how they could do this and be right . . . . [Do] you think that your knowledge . . . is so accurate that you have no fear of having acted impiously?"[73]

To view history as a constantly contestable and contested horizon is no easy thing; but—to employ the *reductio ad Hitlerum*—the only way to prevent the Holocaust from disappearing or being minimized under some new conception of truth is to understand that it *could disappear;* and that preventing it from disappearing means abandoning the idea of universal truth and vigorously defending one's own history, one's place in the struggle. To lose one's history is to lose one's place. Truth will never lack supporters; but politics has higher goals and understands that "the intellectual is not the 'bearer of universal values'"[74] but a gadfly whose task is to contest truth.

In conclusion, then, making history a part of the present political dialogue leads to a major revision of traditional historiography on at least six counts. First, traditional historiography's assumption that history is progress cannot be maintained. If history is naturally progressive and meliorative, there is nothing to argue about. History, however, does not advance like technology. Rather, it is a horizontal never ending series of problems whose origin we in the present constantly dispute and try to rectify. Present problems, therefore, have some core relationship with the past, but one that is always enigmatic, elusive, and subject to multiple interpretations. The task of historians is to present convincing historical arguments about their views of the causes of present difficulties in order to propose solutions to them. In an ideal world, these solutions will be diverse, factious, and asymmetric.

This means, secondly, that the traditional effort of historians to clear their minds of the present in order to see the past more clearly must also be reexamined. A mind totally purged of present considerations, of course, would have no reason to look at history and no means of organizing the eons of events and actors even if it did. But more to the point, if writing history is part of the present political dialogue, then it is precisely today's concerns that should drive the historian's interrogation of the past. In other words, writing history is not a passive, transparent recording of the past but an active effort to compose the past into a meaningful contemporary answer to some social or political problem.

Thirdly, this kind of active political history breaks with traditional history because rather than conducting an impossible search for agreement on the causes of problems peculiar to the present, it attempts to fashion political solutions using historical parallels and equivalents. This implies subordinating an antiquarian interest in the past to the current quest for the conditional good. Because the past is always as enigmatic as the present, the conditional good is never revealed to us as universal or eternal but is something that reveals itself through the current political lens. The challenge, therefore, is to defend one's perspective of history in the constant debate over the meaning of the good, the just, the best means of governing ourselves, defending the country from enemies, punishing crimes, rewarding virtue, educating citizens, and so on.

Hans-Georg Gadamer comes close to this concept with his idea of "effective history" (*Wirkungsgeschichte*); but in the end he eliminates or minimizes conflicting views about the past or the "tradition," as he calls it, by smothering diverse views of the past in an all-encompassing heritage that binds everyone together in the present. Noting that all historical data must be viewed through present "prejudices" Gadamer then suggests that "effective history" involves merging past and present historical "horizons," a process he claims is possible because "we always stand within the tradition"[75] and can, therefore, recall the past. One wonders, however, how such a merging could be anything but an imposition of current views upon the past. How could a person born in the rationalist prejudice of the present understand the religious awe of previous eras? One may surmise the answer by considering the way a rationalist today would explain the behavior of a *contemporary* millennialist. Secondly, it is difficult to see Gadamer's "tradition" as anything other than the prevailing view of historians at a particular time. And how can one who feels oppressed by a prevailing historical fashion share anything with another who feels comfortable with it?[76] Such "sharing" or "mergers" seem suspect, burdened at best by the Enlightenment yearning for a natural law and at worst by the need to enforce conformity against the idiosyncratic and the exceptional.

In contrast to Gadamer then, it seems preferable to recognize that the tradition will never be agreed upon. It will always be individuated and irretrievably buried in layers of interpretation and controversy. To interpret the past, in other words, is always, as Croce suggested, an attempt at advancing an argument about a controversy or difficulty in the present. Such an argument may be employed simply to advance one's own position by creating a noble past for oneself or, as is more fashionable today, by employing the politics of Nietzschean *ressentiment* and deploying an ignoble past to one's perceived oppressor. One need not, however, go as far as Machiavelli in saying that one's interpretation of the past is always only a means of promoting one's own interests.[77] It may, in fact, be an attempt to marshal evidence for one's view about what is best for the whole. In any case, however, the aim of writing/speaking history is to produce an effect in the present.

Fourthly, it follows from the above that a new poetic historiography will replace the traditional historian's concern with verification of sources and determining what really happened with the far more important concern about how to use history to address contemporary problems. In other words, it understands that changes in present political attitudes can only be legitimated by constructing a past that will make the changes credible. For example, for those historians who see contemporary America threatened by dangerous individuals (whether the rich and powerful or the down and out), the already-deployed history that supports an America of individuals with secure *rights* against the majority must be replaced with a different history. Thus, rather than emphasizing the importance of the "individualistic" Bill of Rights, these historians argue that the founders meant to establish a republican *community* with rights against particular individuals and obligations to the whole.[78]

Likewise, the contemporary literature on alterity, the oppressed and the victim, reflects the attempt of the "Other" and their spokesmen to assign a cause for their status that will justify a redress of grievances. This obviously requires the composition of a past different from the one already deployed because that already justifies the present. Thus, George M. Fredrickson, professor of American History at Stanford, arguing for expanded economic benefits for African American citizens, asserts that because "most white Americans believe that blacks [already] enjoy equality of opportunity (or even the edge that affirmative action allegedly provides) and can realize the American dream if they want to," the only way to undermine this belief is to deploy a history that argues that "the unique disabilities imposed on blacks by centuries of slavery and lower-caste status require special measures . . . [T]he open market and normal processes of ethnic assimilation will not suffice."[79]

A necessary corollary to the idea that legitimating any change in the present requires historical justification means that all historical claims must be examined with an eye to what will transpire if the claim becomes accepted as "knowledge." Certainly one can and should defend one's desire to change the present with historical claims; but those with different interests in the present should dispute that history and defend their own history. This political debate, however, will only occur if it is understood that historical claims are present tense and not abstract arguments about the past.

Fifthly, understanding that writing history is a political task gives the past a much more human, poetic, and literary dimension. No longer a record of abstract events or a tail-chasing search for the verifiable cause, historical writing is elevated to a form of political literature that brings past actors and situations into the contemporary human situation. It allows us to listen to and contend with the wisdom of the past, to have earlier voices share in the present debate, and to make historical parallels with present affairs. The ancient poet-historians were right, therefore, to understand that to write history is to compose the past in order to change the present rather than to merely recapitulate exactly what happened. One could certainly ask—and plenty have asked—whether Thucydides, Livy, Ovid, Shakespeare, Vasari, or contemporary historians such as Schama and Carlo Ginzburg "got their facts right." The real question, however, is what were these authors saying about the political issues of their own times and/or about the nature of historical literature.

Bringing history to bear on the present, in other words, makes the remotest events and actors meaningful rather than "historical." The Peloponnesian Wars, the constitution of the Roman Republic, the character of an ancient leader, the nature of Roman slavery and so on can all help us address our own political concerns if they are scrutinized from the present perspective. It is, in other words, only abstractly interesting to pursue traditional history's task of establishing the way that, say, Sophocles' Antigone appeared to ancient Greeks or to see Julius Caesar in the context of Roman history. What is far more useful, and a lot more possible, is to show that Antigone's question of whether she owed more to God or country or the agonizing necessity of ancient Romans in Caesar's time to question their ruler's intentions are not abstract, historical issues, but are relevant to present issues. Understanding the political questions of the past in other words and relating them to the present has a lot more potential for instruction than reading the past for "what really happened."

Finally, by accepting the fact that the past must be viewed from the present rather than from an impossible level of abstract objectivity, one can put past events into a useful context. Unlike traditional history, which claimed only to present a disinterested account, useful history aims at contributing something of political value. As such, it does not distinguish between what really happened and what people believe happened. It recognizes that history can always be put into a context that will advance or retard one's position in the present and that history, therefore, should be judged by what it contributes to the present situation rather its proximity to absolute truth.

We have attributed, in other words, too much to the twilight flight of Hegel's owl. Twilight in history never comes; so one never knows the truth. What matters, as Nietzsche argued in the second of his *Untimely Meditations*, is that history be composed to serve the present good. As such, history is unhistorical. "History, so far as it serves life, serves an unhistorical power." Therefore, it "will not find . . . complete truthfulness to its advantage; it will always approximate, generalize, and finally equate difference," for its purpose is to show that "the great which once existed [may] again be possible."[80] To bring the greatness of the past to life so that it can serve the present and reach into the future is to bring the "soul of historiography" under the dominion of "esthetic criteria" and "closer to fiction." In short, history is, as Nietzsche said of truth, a "mobile army of metaphors, metonyms, and anthropomorphisms"[81] that should be summoned to the current fray.

The essays in this volume are critical of the view that thought can or should explain history with universal historical theory. Unlike

Enlightenment thinkers who believed humans could reason only when they escaped history these essays are suspicious of the eighteenth-century journey to the "state of nature." Certainly the *intent* of clearing the mind of bias was laudable, but stripping humans of their customs, religions, languages, histories, and so on runs the risk of stripping them of their individuality. Instead of the "problem" of different forms of reason, one would have the far greater problem of the mechanical reason of carbon copy "humans."

Instead of seeing "human" reason as the result of purged interest and peculiarities, these essays find humans able to reason only because they are individuals "situated" or "embedded" in their diverse worlds. This particularization of reason accounts for the contemporary interest in language; for to be "situated" in history is to be situated in a local language, the words that a culture has "invented" and constantly updates and revises in its effort to keep up with "things." To learn, therefore, is to learn how to use words a culture, group, or discipline has made. The unvarnished "things themselves" are out of reach, hidden beneath the local cultural "dictionary," where words refer only to other words. It is for this reason that figures such as Vico argue that the only thing one can know for certain is what one has made.

Being confined to this linguistic prism leads to the emphasis in these essays on hermeneutics or interpretation, for if humanity is situated in a historical language, unable to reach absolute knowledge, "thinking" must involve the continuous interpretation and reinterpretation of words. To configure and reconfigure words in an attempt to make them fit a changing world, is what many contemporary thinkers mean by linguistic "play." This "play" requires something beyond or at any rate different from mechanical *ratio* or reason which can only unimaginatively stack and re-stack given meanings.

What is, therefore, most striking about all these essays is the new role given to human imagination and creativity. Imaginative interpretation not only helps us interpret events but, because humans actively respond to new definitions of key words—"history," "rights," "virtue," "justice," "good," and so on—the creation of new meanings, playing with words, produces events, that is, it changes things in the present. Interpretation, therefore, because it involves imagination, leads to an invigorated appreciation for the vast role that art, aesthetics, and *poiesis* play in human society. Therefore, these essays emphasize the poetic nature of much of historical and contemporary reality. The past, in short, constitutes a malleable storehouse of information for *contemporary life* and only by imaginatively reinterpreting the past can one make present truth.

John Nelson, in the first essay in this volume, discusses one of the key ways that humans use poetic language to make or change history. Where I argued in my introductory essay that problems could be addressed though the imaginative redefinition of history, Nelson stresses the importance of updating and redefining key words in order to address present problems. Nelson roots truth in language rather than, as moderns argued, in nature. For Nelson, truth is fundamentally a poetic or imaginative creation that supports the basic institutions and beliefs of the community. The legitimacy of truth, therefore, derives from and rests upon its explicit or implicit acceptance by the community. Once such acceptance is gained, truth is established. But, of course, once truth is established, it becomes the enemy of imagination, the opponent of new truth. The question Nelson, therefore, raises is how can established truth be reinterpreted.

According to Nelson, new or different truths in any culture, text, or discipline—even in the hard sciences—are established by redefining the key words that inform, interconnect, and flow though the system. Nelson calls this redefinition "imaginative etymology." Establishing new definitions can be accomplished by showing that the key words have lost their originally intended meaning. But new meaning can also be produced by demonstrating that the definition of the word at issue is incompatible with the definition of other fundamental words in the system. "Imaginative etymology," in other words, is a means of persuasion, like statistics, charts, and models, that depends upon the ability to creatively weave together key words and concepts into an acceptable, coherent, semantic network.

In the second essay, David Price begins by explaining Nietzsche's idea of moral genealogy, linking it to what the German thinker called "perspectivism." Perspectivism subverts the traditional means of evaluating statements. It implies various points of view and rejects the modern dichotomy that judges everything either "true" or "false." All statements, according to Nietzsche, however strongly they claim to be true, can only be interpretations. This means that readers and auditors of history—and all other texts for that matter—must learn to ask new questions, not whether a statement is true, but why does the writer or speaker interpret matters this way? How will such an interpretation "impact" the reader or listener?

Put this way, art, invention, becomes an essential element of all interpretation; and literature and life thus are closely related. Price then analyzes several examples of the way interpretation of the past constitutes poetic acts suited to the needs of the present: *The Return of Martin Guerre*; *I, Pierre Riviere*; Gananath Obeyesekere's and Marshall Sahlins's conflicting accounts of Captain James Cook's encounter with the Hawaiians; and most importantly, Susan Daitche's novel *L.C.*

On the face of it, *L.C.* is "historical" work, the dairy of Lucienne Crozier, a female participant in the French Revolution of 1848, translated, edited, and introduced—interpreted—by a certain Dr. Willa Rehnfield. According to Rehnfield, the diary relates Lucienne's interpretation of her role in the failed 1848 revolution, her affair with one of the male participants, and her escape to North Africa where she dies of tuberculosis. Rehnfield, a traditional, modern historian, of course, thinks Lucienne's diary is too narrow. She could not know the "real" significance of 1848 because she was too close to the events to understand the "big" picture. Rehnfield, therefore, reinterprets Lucienne's diary, inserting into the interpretation of 1848 established by her peers.

In the midst of the text, however, Rehnfield dies. A second editor, Jane Amme, Rehnfield's assistant appears. She disagrees with Rehnfield's whole interpretation of the diary. Instead of inserting the "diary" into the traditional historical account of the 1848 revolution, Amme rejects Rehnfield's translation of certain key words in the dairy and gives the text a feminist interpretation. It turns out that before becoming an assistant to Rehnfield, Jane Amme was a former 1960s revolutionary, forced to go underground after she killed one Luc Ferrier, a Vietnam war profiteer who raped her. Thus, in *L.C.*, one has Crozier's own interpretation of her experiences and two new interpretations of her original interpretation. In short, *L.C.* illustrates the plasticity of events. And, as with Nelson, it implies that a world that only permits one interpretation would have to outlaw imagination.

Jacqueline LeBlanc's essay discusses the development of Percy Bysshe Shelley's poetic politics. Born the heir of the Enlightenment determination to liberate humanity from poetry and myth and ensure the reign of reason, Shelley eventually became not only one of his age's foremost Romantic poets, but the author of the *Defence of Poetry*, a text which, as LeBlanc puts it, argued that reality or "history itself is a poetic creation." Against the Enlightenment's emphasis on fixed reason, which he eventually concluded had contributed to the Terror of the French Revolution, Shelley sought to stimulate the "poetic imagination," the continuous fashioning of new forms of freedom. Shelley, LeBlanc argues, thus came to anticipate "the Nietzschean conception of history as poiesis, the active *creation* of useful forms of existence."

LeBlanc's essay traces Shelley's career from his early failure as a political activist in Ireland to his subsequent conclusion that poetry was the real force that produced political change. It was the conflict with his rationalist friend, Thomas Love Peacock, LeBlanc argues, that led Shelley to rethink the role of reason, to subordinate politics to poetry, and to understand "politics and history as a system of language and signs."

Unlike fixed reason, poetry lends itself to constant innovation, the reconfiguration through poetic tropes of what "is" into what "can be." The "Ode to the West Wind," LeBlanc argues, was Shelley's metaphor for "poetry itself," the force of "movement" and "change." Reason, on the other hand, because it thrived on permanence, uniformity, and bland homogeneity, lent itself to political repression. Poetry, as the force of imagination and creativity, therefore, is the foundation of human freedom that oppression always fears.

To support freedom, therefore, art must always be open to change. Stephen Brown's "Painting out the Past," however, provides a powerful example of the way art can also be used, or perhaps misused, to support a historical shift to oppressive rigidity. Brown looks at the moment in the career of the painter Jacques-Louis David when he created his revolutionary neoclassical painting, the 1785 *Oath of the Horatii*. It was what was conventionally known as "history painting" and yet its aim was more radical than what that category usually implies, for it intended nothing less than an erasure of history. David would start history anew, going back to a noble Roman past when virtue reigned. In 1785 he was, unknowingly, forecasting the revolutionary calendar of 1794 which would declare a new "Year One." The *Oath* seemed to be a graphic representation of Jean-Jacques Rousseau's attack on the decadent art of pre-Revolutionary France. Against painters such as Fragonard and Boucher, who seemed to make a virtue of sensuality, David called for the reappearance of the militarized virtue that had existed in the ancient Roman republic. Thus, *The Oath of the*

Horatii, Brown argues, meant to "paint out" the corrupt past and take France back to a new beginning. The *Oath* celebrated an exaggerated and grotesque notion of public virtue where any vestige of private interest, even the shared moments of lovers, was regarded as treason and had to be crushed beneath an iron conception of duty to the republic. It was a conception that shortly became all too real in Robespierre's "Republic of Virtue and Terror." And it is not surprising, Brown argues, that David should play an important role supporting Robespierre. Analyzing the form, style, and content of David's painting, Brown shows the way that even great, revolutionary, and creative art can be used to glorify the burial of imagination and the institution of lock-step conformity.

David's painting, therefore, was a usurpation of "factual" history by poetry. Such a process is not foreign to our own times. Brown thus looks at how four contemporary art historians tell the story of David's radical vision. In each case, their versions seem the products of their own times, situations, and circumstances. They see not just David, but David's art and politics through the art and politics of their own times. Brown argues that David, "painting out the past," the modern art historians seeing David through their own lenses, and we ourselves talking about them both, are all participants in a dialogue between our culture and its past. What we call "history" is the crystallization of an instant of this ongoing discourse.

Carole Collier Frick, in her essay, turns to the famous Swiss historian, Jacob Burckhardt, whose famous 1860 *Civilization of the Renaissance*, it is often said, "created" the modern conception we know as the Renaissance. Burkhardt's interpretation/creation of the Renaissance made it the birthplace of modern individualism; and his skill as an interpretive architect made that interpretation the "house" in which Renaissance studies have, until quite recently, lived, or were, perhaps, confined. The question she raises is whether Burckhardt's house is still "useful" today. Can it perhaps be redecorated a bit, or should we move out?

That Burckhardt's interpretation of the Florentine Renaissance was a construct is not, Frick argues, reason enough to start packing. Every epoch, event, or *Weltanschauung* is a construct. As she points out, Burckhardt himself understood that his interpretation was but one of many possible versions of the era. The same era, he said, studied by someone else could easily "receive a wholly different treatment and application" and could lead "to essentially different conclusions." In short, Burkhardt knew he was an artist and that his work was a poetic creation. Rather than submitting it to the old "true/false" dichotomy that Nietzsche, Burckhardt's friend, had rejected, his poetic masterpiece should be measured by present needs.

In Burckhardt's interpretation, the entire Florentine Renaissance was viewed through the prism of art. Everything—diplomacy, Humanism, the State, even warfare—was a manifestation of artistic imagination and creativity. And this imagination and creativity, Burckhardt maintained, was primarily due to Renaissance humanism's interest in the glorification of the worldly individual and its abandonment of the abstract ideas of medieval scholasticism. It is, in fact, this subordination of everything to individualism that accounts for the odd fact that though Burckhardt was fascinated with Renaissance art, he rarely discussed individual art works. It was the artist as individual that interested him.

Burckhardt's vision reflected the interests of a nineteenth-century "art historian interested in *Kultur*," a cultivated gentleman suspicious of the increasing uniformity of modern life. Mid-twentieth-century readers, however, had different fears; and a different dimension of the Renaissance would appeal to them. This dimension was provided with Hans Baron's classic *The Crisis of the Early Italian Renaissance* (1955). Baron, however, did not move out of Burckhardt's palace; he merely redecorated it to suit the tastes of his own time. Thus, he maintained the focus on individualism, but, caught up in the Cold War, he rejected Burckhardt's idea that such individualism could have developed from Humanist thought. It had to have, Baron suggested, a "political" origin. It had developed, he said, as a result of "political and military threat" posed by the power of Milan. Frick then provides several examples of the way art was enlisted in secular political affairs using the paintings of Domenico Ghirlandaio. Finally, she turns to the suggestions of Annalistes, Marxists, feminists, and others that it is time to raze Burckhardt's Renaissance house.

As all these essays indicate, the idea that society is a poetic composition has many dimensions. First, it is the byproduct of the general postmodern condition, belief that truth is not discovered but improvised. Second, where moderns thought imagination was something that clouded the rational vision and should, therefore, be eliminated, postmoderns tend to see even rational thought as a product of imagination. This heightened awareness of individual and collective imagination has made us aware of the way a people's common sense, literature, poetry, art, and other forms of discursive thought determine what kind of truth, knowledge, and sociopolitical institutions a people will find acceptable.

There are, certainly, in this powerful force of imagination some extremely disturbing possibilities. But dreaming that the "truth will out in the end" will not prevent them. Understanding that history is now, as it has always, being used for present purposes may, however, prevent the success of evil interpretations. To be aware that history can take a malign course because of evil interpretation should not, therefore, be seen as an indictment of imagination, but of the right, ability, and duty to use imagination to cope with evil. In any case, if the world and its inhabitants were dominated by fixed truth, then we would not be free to disagree with it. One size would have to fit all. Recognizing that the world has no rational order and that history is not an inevitable progression toward stability is thus a sign of maturity. It constitutes a summons into the real world where danger and chance are everywhere.

NOTES

1. Ever illusive, Socrates uses a *myth* to explain that humans live in a cave of myths and shadows, avoiding the sun that would make the shadows disappear.

2. "Novel Histories," *New York Review of Books,* June 27, 1991, 36.

3. For some recent examples of, and discussion of narrative history, see Hayden White, *Metahistory: The Historical Imagination in Nineteenth Century Europe* (Baltimore: Johns Hopkins University Press, 1973) where the new thinking may well have begun; White, *Tropics of Discourse* (Baltimore: Johns Hopkins University Press, 1978); *The Content of the Form* (Baltimore: Johns Hopkins University Press, 1987); "The Rhetoric of Interpretation," *Poetics Today* 9 (1988): 253–279; "New Historicism: A Comment," *The New Historicism*, ed. J. Aram Veeser (New York: 1989), 293–302; *I, Pierre Rivière, having slaughtered my mother, my sister and my brother . . . : A Case of Parricide in the 19th Century*, ed. Michel Foucault, trans. Frank Jellinek (New York: Pantheon Books, 1975); Carlo Ginzburg, *The Cheese and the Worms: The Cosmos of a Sixteenth-Century Miller* (Baltimore: Johns Hopkins University Press 1980); Na-

talie Zemon Davis, *The Return of Martin Guerre* (Cambridge: Harvard University Press, 1983); Jonathan Spence, *The Question of Hu* (New York: Knopf, 1988); Robert Rosenstone, *Mirror in the Shrine: American Encounters with Meiji Japan* (Cambridge: Harvard University Press, 1988); Simon Schama, *Dead Certainties: Unwarranted Speculations* (New York: Knopf, 1991); Richard Holmes, *Dr. Johnson and Mr. Savage* (New York: Pantheon, 1993); David Hackett Fischer, *Paul Revere's Ride* (New York: Oxford University Press, 1994); and the ongoing discussions in the journal *History and Theory*.

4. *Citizens: A Chronicle of the French Revolution* (New York: Vintage, 1990), xiii.

5. *Citizens*, xvi.

6. *The Late Mattia Pascal*, trans. William Weaver (New York: Eridanos Press, 1987), 256.

7. For example, Plato (c.427–c.347 B.C.), Vico (1668–1744), Rousseau (1712–1778), and Hegel (1770–1831).

8. Giambattista Vico, *The New Science*, trans. Thomas Goddard Bergin and Max Harold Fisch (Ithaca: Cornell University Press, 1984), parag. 379.

9. De Sanctis, as quoted in *Antonio Gramsci: Quaderni del carcere*, ed. Valentino Gerratana Vols. I–IV (Turin: Einaudi, 1975): III, 2185–86 (My translation).

10. See Vico, *The New Science*, Book III.

11. Vico, *New Science*, parag. 965; Michael Crawford, "Early Rome and Italy," *The Oxford History of the Classical World*, ed. John Boardman et al. (Oxford: Oxford University Press, 1986), 387–417, noted (396) that "at Rome religion and politics were not two worlds, but inseparable parts of the same world." This is also maintained by Karl Christ: "The continual close contact with the gods was for the Romans not only a private matter but likewise a political affair of state. Before an important political occasion . . . the will of the gods was ascertained by observations of the sky, analysis of the flight of birds, or examination of entrails. . . . Owing to the close interconnections between religion and politics, the sacral domain could not be separated from one which was profane but also political." *The Romans* (Berkeley: University of California Press, 1985), 159.

12. The Romans, for example, saw law as the word of God, the *religio verborum* that in early Roman society was displayed as a song, incantation, or formula (*carmen*), even—as Livy put it (*History*, I xxvi 5)—a dread song, a "*Lex horrendi carminis*." Long ago, Sir Philip Sidney noted the religious orientation of early life: "Among the Romans," said Sidney, "a poet was called *vates*, which is as much as a diviner, foreseer, or prophet. . . . May not I presume a little further to show the reasonableness of this word *vates*, and say that the holy David's Psalms are a divine poem?" Like the Psalms, the prophecies of the Oracles of Delphos and Sibylla were also, Sidney noted, "delivered in verses . . . [and

seemed] to have some divine force in [them]." "A defense of Poesy," *Critical Theory Since Plato*, ed. Hazard Adams (New York: Harcourt Brace Janovich, 1971), 156–157.

13. Ernst Breisach, *Historiography: Ancient, Medieval, and Modern* (Chicago: University of Chicago Press, 1994), 126. The *trivium* led to the Bachelor of Arts degree and included grammar, logic, and rhetoric; while students of the *quadrivium* of arithmetic, geometry, astronomy, and music attained the Master of Arts.

14. Thus, in introducing his history of Rome, Livy made no effort to find out whether or not the legends of the past were true, but instead urged his contemporaries to read the legends in order to see what the men and morals were like when Rome was founded—and to then reflect how "with the gradual relaxation of discipline, morals first gave way, as it were, then sank lower and lower, finally began the downward plunge which has brought us to the present time" (*History*, Bk.I: Preface). Likewise, Plutarch, whose works are essentially moral exhortations supported by legend, did not ask whether his legends were true because, as he noted in his essay on Pericles, historical "truth . . . is hard to capture by research, since those who come after the events . . . find that lapse of time . . . an obstacle . . . while . . . [one's] contemporaries . . . , partly through envious hatred and partly through fawning flattery, defile and distort the truth." (*Lives*, trans. Bernadette Perrin [Loeb Classical Library, Cambridge: Harvard University Press, 1967], 47). So uninterested in scientific history were the ancients that Collingwood found it odd that figures such as Herodotus and Thucydides even bothered with the idea; for according to Greek thought, what mattered was the "constant" while, "change"—time or history—could not be known. See, R.G. Collingwood, *The Idea of History* (New York: Galaxy Press, 1956), 20ff.

15. Francis M. Cornford agreed—though he considered their lack of science a failing—and accused Thucydides of being a mere poet rather than a historian. See *Thucydides Mythistoricus* (Philadelphia: University of Pennsylvania Press, 1971), 52ff. On the history of historiography, see Breisach, *Historiography: Ancient, Medieval, and Modern.*

16. J. G. A.Pocock, *The Machiavellian Moment: Florentine Political Thought and the Atlantic Republican Tradition* (Princeton: Princeton University Press, 1975), 31.

17. J. G. A. Pocock, *Machiavellian Moment*, 49.

18. Edward Gibbon, *The Decline and the Fall of the Roman Empire*, ed. J.B. Bury (New York: The Heritage Press, 1946), Vol. I, 24.

19. *Republic*, trans. Allan Bloom (New York: Basic Books, 1968), 607b. (my emphasis).

20. *The Peloponnesian Wars*, trans. Richard Crawley, rev. R. Fleetham (Chicago: University Press, 1952), 1.21.

21. Ibid., I. 22.

22. Aristotle, *Poetics*, 51b1–11: "The historian and the poet do not differ according to whether they write in verse or without verse. . . . The difference is that the former relates things that have happened, the latter things that may happen. F*or this reason poetry is a more philosophical and a more serious thing than history*; poetry tends to speak of universals, history of particulars. A universal is the sort of thing that a certain kind of person may well say or do in accordance with probability or necessity. . . . A particular is what Alcibiades did or what he suffered." (my emphasis)

23. For discussion of some of the extended meanings of poetry, see Eric Havelock, *The Liberal Temper in Greek Politics* (London, 1957); *Preface to Plato* (Cambridge: Harvard University Press, 1963); *The Literate Revolution in Greece and its Cultural Consequences* (Princeton: Princeton University Press, 1982); Werner Jaeger, *Paideia*, trans. Gilbert Highet (New York: Oxford University Press, 1960), 3 Vols; George Kennedy, *The Art of Persuasion in Greece* (Princeton: Princeton University Press: 1963); Walter J. Ong, S.J., *Orality and Literacy: The Technologizing of the Word* (New York: Methuen, 1982); Brian Vickers, *In Defense of Rhetoric* (Oxford: Clarendon Press, 1990).

24. See, Isocrates, *Nicocles* 5–9 in Werner Jaeger, *Paideia*, II: 89. Cicero, *De Inventione*, 1. 2. 2. It is, of course, the main theme of the *New Science* and of Machiavelli's advice that, because men are still primitive and half-bestial, a successful ruler must be like Chiron, half-man and half-beast. See *Prince* 18, for example.

25. Gordon Wood, "Novel History," 31 and 34.

26. Derrida calls this "modern" thought "logocentric" for its *assumption* that there is a *reason* or *logos* in everything and that humans can know it. To emphasize the sectarian nature of such thought, he calls it "nothing but the most original and powerful ethnocentrism." *Of Grammatology*, trans. Gayatri Chakravorty Spivak (Baltimore: Johns Hopkins University Press, 1976), 3. The myth of the *logos*, for Derrida, was, like the myth of the ancient poets, simply a convention written in logical script. Martin Heidegger, to cite only the most accessible of his works, sees reason, *ratio*, and logic as a "technological" form of reasoning ("The Question Concerning Technology," in *The Question Concerning Technology and Other Essays*, trans. William Lovitt [New York: Harper and Row, 1977], 3–35) that began as early as Parmenides and constituted a (vain) effort to exorcize frightening "fate" or *Moira* from reality. See, "Moira (Parmenides VIII, 34–41)," in Heidegger, *Early Greek Thinking: The Dawn of Modern Philosophy*, trans. David Farrell Krell and Frank A. Capuzzi (New York: Harper and Row, 1984), 79–101.

27. For example (and despite their many differences) Hans Baron, *The Crisis of the Early Italian Renaissance* (Princeton: Princeton University Press, 1968); William J. Bouwsma, *Venice and the Defense of Republican Liberty* (Berke-

ley: University of California Press, 1968); Ernst Cassirer, *The Myth of the State* (New Haven: Yale University Press, 1946); Eugenio Garin, *Medioevo e Rinascimento* (Bari: Laterza, 1954); George Holmes, *The Florentine Enlightenment: 1400–1450* (New York: Pegasus, 1969); Erwin Panofsky, *Renaissance and Renascences in Western Art* (Stockholm: 1960); J.G.A. Pocock, *The Machiavellian Moment*; Quentin Skinner, *The Foundations of Modern Political Thought*, 2 Vols. (Cambridge: Cambridge University Press, 1978).

28. Max Weber, in *The Protestant Ethic and the Spirit of Capitalism* (New York: Scribner, 1958), and *The Theory of Social and Economic Organizations*, trans. Talcott Parsons (London: With. Hodge, 1947) and elsewhere, saw modern society as the place where the individual emerges as autonomous or "unsituated" but paradoxically then finds himself enmeshed in an "iron cage" of rational bureaucracy. On Weber, see Gunther Roth and Wolfgang Schluchter, *Max Weber's Vision of History: Ethics and Methods* (Berkeley: University of California Press, 1979) and Lawrence A. Scaff, *Fleeing the Iron Cage: Culture, Politics, and Modernity in the Thought of Max Weber* (Berkeley: University of California Press, 1991). Jean-Francois Lyotard, *The Postmodern Condition: A Report on Knowledge*, trans. Geoff Bennington and Brian Massumi (Minneapolis: University of Minnesota Press, 1984) locates the emergence of a rational "metanarrative" in the birth of the scientific outlook on the world; Michel Foucault, explores some of the implications of this arbitrary metanarrative or "episteme," as he calls it, in almost all of his works. A good beginning is *Madness and Civilization: A History of Insanity in the Age of Reason*, trans. Richard Howard (New York: Vintage, 1973). More difficult is *The Order of Things: The Archeology of the Human Sciences* (New York: Vintage, 1973). See too, Timothy J. Reiss, *The Discourse of Modernism* (Ithaca: Cornell University Press, 1982). One characteristic of modernity then, is the belief that the individual can attain an objective view of human and natural things by abstracting the self from history and becoming what Peter Berger, Brigitte Berger, and Hansfried Kellner call *The Homeless Mind*. ([New York: Vintage Books, 1974]; and Berger, *Facing up to Modernity* [New York, Basic Books, 1977]). The idea of the "homeless mind" (roughly, Heidegger's *Unheimlichkeit*) is often associated with the Enlightenment idea of man in the "state of nature." Against the modern view of the "homeless mind," postmodern thought often aims at re-situating humans into history, a major theme of the works of Martin Heidegger in, for example, *Being and Time*, trans. John Macquarrie and Edward Robinson (New York: Harper and Row, 1962) and of scholars like Robert Bellah et al. *Habits of the Heart: Individualism and Commitment in American Life* (Berkeley: University of California Press, 1985); Michael J. Sandel, *Liberalism and the Limits of Justice* (Cambridge: Cambridge University Press, 1982) and others.

29. It is difficult to overestimate the impact of Cartesian algebraic or analytic geometry; for it was not abstract, but allowed *physical* forms in the world to be written in *algebraic* script rather than in the clumsy geometry the Greeks had used. Newton's and Leibniz's even more amazing discovery of the calculus allowed the algebraic description of even accelerating physical bodies. All this seemed to indicate that man and nature had at last found a common language.

30. Convinced that knowledge could defeat chance, Pierre Simon Laplace, the author of the five volume *Celestial Mechanics* (1799–1825), held that were one to have at hand the laws of physics and knowledge of every body's position and velocity at a particular instant, it would be possible, in principle, to know the exact location of all bodies past and future. In short, everything operated according to rational and discoverable laws. Heisenberg's later discovery of particle indeterminacy reduced this absolute certainty to statistical probability; but it left intact the scientific conviction that chance was much less significant than regularity. Only with the emergence of chaos theory has this idea been questioned.

31. As Edward Said noted, "The best example of what a lay science could and could not do was provided . . . by Renan in a lecture at the Sorbonne in 1878, 'On the Services Rendered by Philology to the Historical - Sciences.' What is revealing about this text is the way Renan clearly had religion in mind when he spoke about philology—for example, what philology, like religion, teaches us about the origins of humanity, civilization and language. . . . The only way in which [Renan] could move out of religion into philological scholarship was to retain in the new lay science the historical world-view he had gained from religion." *Orientalism* (New York: Vintage, 1979), 134–135.

32. Thomas Buckle, *The History of Civilization in England*, in *The Varieties of History*, ed. Fritz Stern (New York, World Publishing Co., 1966), 127. Buckle's aim was to use statistics to account for the "superiority of [Europe] over other parts of the world" for, though statistics was "still in its infancy, [it] has already thrown more light on the study of human nature than all the sciences put together." And the statistics revealed that Europe's superiority came from the fact "the tendency has been, in Europe, to subordinate nature to man; out of Europe, to subordinate man to nature." Buckle, "History and the Operation of Universal Laws," in *Theories of History*, ed Patrick Gardiner (New York: The Free Press, 1959), 119–120. Statistics is a wonderful thing. Someone once calculated that the safest place to wheel a baby carriage is down the middle of a superhighway because, statistically speaking, very few babies are killed that way.

33. Leopold von Ranke, *Histories of the Latin and Germanic Nations from 1494–1514* in Stern, 57.

34. Ranke, "A fragment from the 1860's," in Stern, *Varieties,* 61–62. The idea is hardly dead. Thus, Collingwood observed that, "the modern historian knows that if only he had the capacity he could become the interpreter of the whole past of mankind"; that "nowadays we think of monographs on various subjects as ideally forming part of a universal history"; and "in analyzing the thought of a philosopher, just as in analyzing, say, a political situation, one will always find incoherences and contradictions; *these contradictions are always between retrograde and progressive elements*; and it is of the utmost importance, if we are to make anything of our analysis, to distinguish correctly which are the progressive elements and which the retrograde. The great merit of studying our subject historically is that it enables us to make this distinction with certainty." *The Idea of History*, 25–27; 135, emphasis added.

35. The whole of James Joyce's *Ulysses,* for example.

36. *Reason in History*, trans. Robert Hartman (Indianapolis: Bobbs-Merrill, 1953), 11.

37. Not everyone, however, was so optimistic. Thinkers like Oswald Spengler (1880–1936) and Arnold J. Toynbee (1889–1975), for example, saw history as an infinite series of historical cycles. All civilizations have a period of growth, maturity, and eventual decline. The cyclical principle, employed earlier by thinkers such as Vico and Machiavelli and still earlier by Roman historians like Livy, Sallust, and Tacitus, was not so much deterministic as tragic: If a civilization was lucky enough to survive through its early and most vulnerable stages, and if it forged the necessary moral and physical determination and savagery to defeat its most threatening enemies, it was still doomed; for triumph inevitably led to "refinement" and the physical and moral disarmament that rendered the once victorious people vulnerable to an attack by others at an earlier stages of development. The fact that all people went through the same cycle led Toynbee to conclude that because every society experienced the same moral rise and fall, the experiences of preceding societies were relevant to our own. Indeed, as he put it, "on the time-scale now unfolded by geology and cosmogony, the five or six thousand years that had elapsed since the first emergence of . . . human society . . . were [so] infinitesimally brief [that we are all] one another's contemporaries" anyway. Toynbee, *Civilization on Trial* and *The World and West* (New York: Meridian Books, 1959), 19.

38. A general account of this entire process is in Stephen Toulmin, *Cosmopolis: The Hidden Agenda of Modernity* (New York: The Free Press, Macmillan, 1990).

39. Edward Gibbon, *The Decline and Fall*, I, 60.

40. It is a definition of reason and history, as many have pointed out, that leaves room for a lot of mischief; for with the advance of reason and narrowing of choice, freedom must necessarily decrease.

41. And according to some, maybe the end was not that far off. As Daniel C. Dennett put it in 1991, "[After] I read Descartes's *Meditations*, [I became] hooked on the mind-body problem. . . . How on earth could my thoughts and feelings fit in the same world with the nerve cells and molecules that made up my brain? Now, after thirty years of thinking, talking and writing about this mystery, I think . . . I can sketch an outline of the solution, a theory of consciousness that gives answers . . . to the questions that have been just as baffling to philosophers and scientists as to laypeople." *Consciousness Explained* (Boston: Little Brown & Co., 1991), xi.

42. See Steven J. Hawking, *A Brief History of Time: From the Big Bang to Black Holes* (Bantam: New York, 1990), 156.

43. *Cartesian Meditations: An Introduction to Phenomenology*, trans. Dorion Cairns (The Hague: Martinus Nijoff, 1970), 7.

44. An excellent exploration of the way the eighteenth century dispensed with the fundamental truths of the *ancien regime* prior to and during the French Revolution, however, is in the following: Francois Furet, *Interpreting the French Revolution* (Cambridge: Cambridge University Press, 1981); Lynn Hunt, *Politics, Culture, and Class in the French Revolution* (Berkeley: University of California Press, 1984); Carol Blum, *Rousseau and The Republic of Virtue: Language and Politics in the French Revolution* (Ithaca: Cornell University Press, 1986); William Doyle, *Origins of the French Revolution* (Oxford: Oxford University Press, 1988; *The French Revolution and the Creation of Modern Political Culture*, vol. I, ed. Keith Michael Baker (Oxford: Oxford University Press, 1987), vol. II, ed. Colin Lucas (Oxford: Oxford University Press, 1991); *Fictions of the French Revolution*, ed. Bernadette Fort (Evanston: Northwestern University Press, 1991).

45. That *other* organisms—viruses, bacteria, and parasites—might continue to evolve, adapting and reshaping themselves into life-forms with payloads deadly enough and drug-resistant enough to make *themselves* the "fittest," used to seem unthinkable. No longer. See, for example, Laurie Garrett, *The Coming Plague: Newly Emerging Diseases in a World out of Balance* (New York: Penguin, 1995) which, despite the popularized title and ideological baggage, gives a fine account of the on-going contest we call the "survival of the fittest."

46. Thus, after concluding his long relationship with Marxism, Eugene Genovese remarked that after "a seventy year experiment with socialism [he and his fellow Marxists had] little more to our credit than tens of millions of

corpses." Quoted in David Brion Davis, "Southern Comfort," *New York Review of Books* (Oct. 5, 1995), 43.

47. As well as at least nine other books, the most well-known of which are: *Prophecy Deliverance! An Afro-American Revolutionary Christianity* (1982); *Breaking Bread: Insurgent Black Intellectual Life* (1991); *Beyond Eurocentrism and Multiculturalism*, I, II,(1993); *Keeping Faith: Philosophy of Race in America* (1993).

48. Alasdair MacIntyre, *After Virtue*: *A Study in Moral Theory* (Notre Dame University of Notre Dame Press, 1981), 2, 4, and see also 48 and 70. Robert N. Bellah et al., *Habits of the Heart: Individualism and Community in American Life* (New York: Harper and Row, Perrenial Library, 1985), 114–115; 284; 295–296. Robert Heilbronner, "Lifting the Silent Depression," *New York Review of Books* (October 24, 1991), 6. Cornel West, "Afterword: The Politics of American Neo-Pragmatism" in *Post-Analytic Philosophy*, ed. John Rajchman and Cornel West (New York, Columbia University Press, 1985), 259–272, see 259. Leo Strauss, "An Epilogue," in *Essays on The Scientific Study Of Politics*, ed. Herbert J. Storing (New York: Holt, Rinehart and Winston, Inc. 1962), 307–327, 327. Francis Fukuyama, *The End of History and the Last Man* (New York: Macmillan, 1992), 3–4 and 305ff. Martin Heidegger, ""Only a God Can Save Us': *Der Spiegel*'s interview with Martin Heidegger (1966)" in *The Heidegger Controversy: A Critical Reader*, ed. Richard Wolin (Cambridge: MIT Press, 1993), 91–116.

49. Jean-Francois Lyotard, *The Postmodern Condition*, xxiv.

50. Common sense, or *Sensus communis*, is a key term in Vico, who explains in the *New Science*, "Human choice, by its nature most uncertain, is made certain and determined by the common sense of men. . . . Common sense is judgement without reflection, shared by an entire class, an entire people, an entire nation, or the entire human race" (parags. 141 and 142).

51. Thus, Foucault refers to the idea of a natural order as a mere "Western" episteme, Derrida as the "transcendental signifier," Heidegger as an arbitrary "framework."

52. Unlike Thales and the moderns, however, Ferris, author of nine books, more than a hundred articles, and having taught in four disciplines, is under no illusions about the mysteries of the universe. See *The Whole Shebang: A State of the Universe(s) Report* (New York: Simon and Schuster, 1997).

53. See, for example, *Nature's Imagination: The Frontiers of Scientific Vision*, ed. John Cornwall (Oxford: Oxford University Press, 1994) with an introduction by no less than Freeman Dyson, one of the architects of quantum electrodynamics. It is, of course, hard to discover the genealogy of something this complex. Kuhn's book was published in 1962 and Lyotard's essay in 1979. But the cat was already out of the bag in 1927 with Martin Heidegger's *Being*

and Time, which showed the way humans had ignored the *Seinsfrage*, the "Being Question"; that is, humans had from the beginning assumed that Being was a thing, a substance, like Thales's water, rather than a human construct that prefigured the way humans saw the world of beings.

54. Kuhn, *Structure of Scientific Revolutions* (Chicago: University of Chicago Press, 1962), 11, 62.

55. *Critique of Pure Reason*, trans. Norman Kemp Smith (New York: St. Martins Press, 1965), 20.

56. Kuhn, *The Essential Tension: Selected Studies in Scientific Tradition and Change* (Chicago: University of Chicago Press, 1977).

57. The titles alone give the flavor of these texts on the "hard" sciences: Paul Feyerabend, *Farewell to Reason* (London: Verso, 1988); John L. Casti, *Paradigms Lost: Tackling the Unanswered Mysteries of Modern Science* (New York: Avon, 1989); James Gleick, *Chaos: Making a New Science* (New York: Penguin, 1988). Of course, it has also attracted the spirited opposition of reductionists like Steven Weinberg, Stephen Hawking, and many others.

58. All quoted from Gleick, *Chaos*, 6.

59. Gould, *Wonderful Life: The Burgess Shale and the Nature of History* (New York: Norton, 1989).

60. Prigogine and Isabelle Stengers, *Order out of Chaos: Man's New Dialogue with Nature* (New York: Bantam, 1984), xi–xxxi, 4, 301ff.

61. An excellent introduction to this new history is Lynn Hunt's "Introduction" to *The New Cultural History*, ed. Lynn Hunt (Berkeley: University of California Press, 1989), 1–22.

62. Foucault's writings and especially those of Derrida are sometimes counterexamples of the old adage that "*Ce qui n'est pas clair n'est pas francais.*" They are, in short, not for the faint of heart. Derrida's *Of Grammatology*, trans. Gayatri Chakravorty Spivak (Baltimore: Johns Hopkins University Press, 1976) and *Writing and Difference*, trans. Alan Bass (Chicago: University of Chicago Press, 1978) are excellent introductions. The *Derrida Reader: Between the Blinds*, ed. Peggy Kamuf (New York: Columbia, 1991) is a fine guide to some of the more daunting writings. Foucault is usually less formidable, but may have the most sophisticated notion of power since Nietzsche. Good overviews of his ideas are in his "introduction" to *The Archaeology of Knowledge*, trans. A.M. Sheridan Smith (New York: Harper and Row, 1972), 3–17 and in the interview "Truth and Power," in *Power/Knowledge: Selected Interviews and other Writings (1972–1977)*, ed. and trans. Colin Gordon et al. (New York: Pantheon, 1980), 109–133. More difficult, but well worth it is *The Order of Things: The Archeology of the Human Sciences* (New York: Random House, 1973).

63. Derrida, "Positions," trans. Allan Bass (Chicago: University of Chicago Press, 1982), 41ff.

64. Indeed, one of Foucault's most challenging texts is *Lets Mots et Choses*. The English edition is *The Order of Things: An Archaeology of the Human Sciences*, no translator given (New York: Vintage, 1973).

65. For example, in *The Order of Things*, 303–387, especially 312.

66. "Nietzsche, Genealogy, History," trans. Donald F. Bouchard and Sherry Simon, in *The Foucault Reader*, ed. Paul Rabinow (New York: Penguin, 1987), 76–100, quotes from 86–88.

67. *Citizens*, 281 and 268.

68. See e.g., the works of Keith Michael Baker, Carole Blum, William Doyle, and Francois Furet.

69. "How did reason come into the world?" asks Nietzsche. "As is fitting, in an irrational manner, by accident." *Dawn*, 123 in *The Portable Nietzsche*, trans. Walter Kaufman (New York: Penguin, 1968), 81.

70. The late Francois Furet, one of the most brilliant pioneers of post-Marxist revisionism in the study of the French Revolution, as quoted in Lynn Hunt, "Introduction," *New Cultural History*, 9.

71. *La storia come pensiero e come azione* (Bari: Laterza, 1966), 9, 11, 27. (my translation)

72. Ranke, "A Fragment from the 1860's," in Stern, *Varieties*, 61–62.

73. *Euthyphro*, 4b–e.

74. "Truth and Power," in *Power/Knowledge*, 131–132.

75. *Truth and Method*, ed. Garrett Borden and John Cumming (New York: Crossroads Publishing Co. 1984), 267ff, 305ff.

76. See for example Foucault, *The Order of Things* (New York: Random House, Vintage, 1970), preface, xv.

77. Machiavelli, like Croce, suggests that history is always focused on the present and often is nothing more than the inventions (or illusions) of the ambitious. As he put it in *Discourses* 2.5, the world had existed forever and historical records had been destroyed by humans and by heaven so many times that a truly accurate recovery of the past was out of the question. What passes for history is simply the rhetoric of aggressive and determined men who "hide or pervert" the past "to gain a name and reputation for themselves" in the present (*per farsi ripulazione e nome, la nasconde, e la perverte a suo modo*). (my translation)

78. See, for example, Sheldon Wolin, "Revolutionary Action Today," in *Post-Analytic Philosophy*, ed. Rajchman and West, 244–257; J. G. A. Pocock, *The Machiavellian Moment*, Bellah, et al. *Habits of the Heart*, but especially, Bellah, *The Broken Covenant: American Civil Religion in the Time of Trial* (Chicago: University of Chicago Press, 2nd ed, 1992); Michael J Sandel, *Democracy's Discontent: America in Search of a Public Philosophy* (Cambridge: Harvard University Press, 1996).

79. Fredrickson, "Land of Opportunity?" *The New York Review of Books* (April 4, 1996), 4.

80. *On the Advantage and Disadvantage of History for Life*, trans. Peter Preuss (Indianapolis: Hackett, 1988), 14–17.

81. "On Truth and Lie," in *The Portable Nietzsche*, 46.

CHAPTER ONE

Imaginative Etymology (As a Type of Evidence and a Trope of Argument)

John S. Nelson

Words are the source of misunderstandings.

—Antoine de Saint-Exupery

In the late-modern academy, we celebrate the distrust of language as the beginning of method. Method, we know, is what makes any inquiry reliable, testable, truthful, progressive. And scientific method, the methodology textbooks tell us, must start in *conceptualization*: careful specification of the meaning(s) of key terms. Precision at the outset can help us to exclude unwanted meanings. We stipulate the sense intended, then specify the operations for measuring the concept that results; and we might even name it anew, coining some neologism. (Never mind that to specify the definitions and operations is to express them in still other words, which themselves cannot receive such special treatment—upon pain of an infinite regress. Nor should we worry that any new word can label intelligibly only to the extent that scientists can and do translate it into some existing terms.) Though there is no escape from language when we face communication among scientists, let alone politicos or ordinary people, still there is real protection in the rigorous articulation of terms encouraged by such procedures.

This methodological protection must be especially urgent for the sciences of society, since they address objects embedded intrinsically in language. Social phenomena come already laden with words, because many happen in speech and the rest appear in social situations sculpted of language. To resist the siren songs of meaning in ordinary words, therefore, late-modern scientists of society must be even more vigilant and clever than their counterparts in the purely natural or formal sciences. Thus, social scientists must know well their words, but only as puritans must know well their sins: to escape them where possible and, where not, to minimize and repent of their damage. Indeed, social scientists must study the polysemy of words, to combat their invidious effects on the souls of their sciences, but they may not rejoice in the slippery richness of language.

Only humanists and literati would revel in the playful nuances or historical dimensions of words. Sometimes such people seem to study the same subjects; but social scientists know that these critics, novelists, playwrights, and poets lack rigor in their procedures of inquiry and communication. Always the two camps must share entanglement in words, since social scientists too must write and talk, but proper scientists know that humanists and "writers" are unsystematic in their evidence—if, indeed, they may be said to deal in evidence at all. Words are the last places a modern scientist would look for good evidence about social phenomena.

Or are they? Contrary to the conventional wisdom, the arguments of social scientists rely often and crucially on evidence from several kinds of disciplined play with the meanings of words. Even in the most rigorous modes imaginable, I would argue, the conceptualization and operationalization of the social sciences involve the play of meanings. This first kind of dependence on words must remain a case for another occasion, but some of my colleagues in the social sciences might think the point a modest concession at most. The official purpose of conceptualization, after all, is to confine the play of meanings to one step in the scientific method—limiting the perverse powers of words to a single, separate context where they can receive special scrutiny.

More remarkable, perhaps, is the reliance of some work throughout the social sciences on arguments from etymology. Then the histories of word usage become evidence for various claims about human action. Thus, histories of *participation* and *voting* can figure into social-scientific arguments about how to explain the turnout patterns in an election, how to describe the political mobilizations of a populace, or how to the measure the economic conditions for a revolution. But again a staunch social scientist might minimize the significance of the point. Express turns to etymology as historical evidence are not now prominent in the social sciences, I must admit, save for the small subfields devoted directly to historical and normative questions. By marginalizing these subfields, furthermore, modernist social sciences strive to make them the exceptions that prove the recent rule: that words and meanings make bad evidence, deserving suspicion rather than respect.

Yet social scientists cannot dismiss or minimize the importance of a third kind of word evidence in their inquiry. Though it offends outrageously the official, modernist canons of evidence, this play with the powers of words contributes mightily to persuading social scientists (plus politicians, judges, lawyers, laymen, and the like) to accept some of their most prominent arguments. Nearly unnoticed, such power plays with language even help to secure allegiance to several of the presently paradigmatic styles of research in the social sciences. Shared with the humanities, such evidence seems all the harder to legitimate because it is more imaginative than historical. Its historical warrants are often weak and always peripheral to its success. On striking occasions, it even defies historical usages to persuade instead by configuring large bodies of data and reasons in useful ways. This is the type of evidence which we may call imaginative etymology. My adventurous thesis is that imaginative or poetic etymology is a legitimate form of evidence and a valuable trope of argument—in the social sciences as well as the humanities. Imaginative etymology puts the postmodern power of myth and poetry into historical persuasion throughout the human sciences.

Words, Words, Everywhere, and Many a Meaning to Each

> The best explanation of a word is often that which is suggested by its derivation. . . . There are cases, in which more knowledge of more value may be conveyed by the history of a word, than by the history of a campaign.
>
> —Samuel Taylor Coleridge

Dictionaries treat etymologies as exercises in history. What we regard as an ordinary etymology, therefore, is a documentable account of linguistic change. It tells the derivation of a word or its evolution in meaning. By contrast, an imaginative etymology invents a plausible account of a concept crucial to some substantive argument. To recognize imaginative etymologies as devices of argument is useful but not enough: we also must acknowledge them as potentially valid evidence. And to do that requires an exercise in the poetics—as well as the rhetorics—of argumentation.

Imaginative etymologies often stem from poetic inspection of a word's apparent structure or elements. If iron ages are situations of terrible trouble, then perhaps *iron-y* is a figure of language and life especially fit for coping with troubled times.[1] If a *com-promise* is a *promise-with*, a *promise-in-common*, or a *promise-shared*,[2] then perhaps a *comm-unity* is a *unity-with*, a *unity-through-commonality*, or *unity-with-respect-to-what-we-share*.[3] These imaginative etymologies readily give rise (or at least give voice) to provocative, useful theories of irony, compromise, and community—not only as words but also as phenomena. Historical etymologists would tell us that only the middle etymology of compromise is a factually defensible derivation. (At any rate, this is what they say at the moment: the judgments of historical etymologists have been known to change, depending on new textual evidence and new imaginative connections.) By strict historical standards, the other two "etymologies" are made up, imaginary, false. Yet all three contribute to good arguments in several fields. Imaginative etymologies need not be mere mistakes of history; they can be valid devices of argument.

Rhetoricians of inquiry focus on what actually persuades specific audiences, especially in the academy. Thus, Deirdre McCloskey shows that many an economist's argument depends more on appeals usually classified as "literary" than on considerations generally regarded as "scientific" in some harder sense.[4] The point is not to discredit economists; it is to invalidate their inaccurate, scientistic contrast between "literary" and "scientific" arguments. More sensitive to their actual dynamics of argument, economists can learn better how to improve their inquiries.[5]

Not to renounce but to improve our uses of imaginative etymology: this is the main reason to recognize its poetic importance in arguments throughout the social sciences. To be sure, it has seldom been noticed as such by writers or readers in the humanities, let alone in the social sciences. Were it acknowledged, however, more than a few analysts of argument would misclassify it as a fallacy—perhaps calling it *false etymology*. Thus, John Ciardi, that grumpy lover of words, used to boil with outrage about the "spook etymologists" who derive their meanings from spurious, pseudo-etymological fabrications of word histories.

Some philosophers of evidence might deny even "true etymology" a respectable role in substantive argument, at least in arguments about so-called "empirical questions." Dismissing matters of etymology as merely semantic or conceptual, rather than empirical, these standard-setters would condemn invocations of historical etymology as commissions of "the etymological fallacy." And some social scientists would extend this fallacy to cover any use of etymology in addressing warrants for their technical concepts. Surely, they would say, the histories of ordinary words are largely irrelevant to the uses of technical concepts with stipulated meanings—even if these share the same name. If the goal of conceptualization is to avoid confusing new definitions with old meanings, then what strange conception of evidence would let old usages test our applications of newly operationalized categories?

These accusations against etymology depend on the philosophical dichotomy between the logical or conceptual (form or reasons) and the empirical or substantive (evidence or contents). After Wittgenstein and Quine, however, we have ample reasons for rejecting this dichotomy.[6] After the structuralists, moreover, we should know better than to treat any terms as meaningful in complete separation from their contexts: words mean in networks of discourse, rather than as atoms of speech.[7] And if that were not enough, we also have the several "new histories" in political theory, literature, and other domains—telling us how speech paradigms construct the social objects and meanings of their disparate times.[8]

In all these endeavors, there has been a concern (often unaware and unsystematic but important in the details) to escape a homogenizing (Hegelian) preoccupation of intellectual history with "perennial issues" and patterns of "continuity versus innovation." In place of the history of ideas, the new historians study paradigms of language, epistemes of concepts, and discourses of rhetoric. They are interested in how ways of thinking, talking, and acting cohere.[9] Some study as well how they appear and disappear. Some of these new historians turn overtly poetic, favoring the "archaeology of knowledge" or the "genealogy of discourse" over the (old) history of (high, elite) ideas.[10] The new historicism in literary studies is more prosaic, arising to counteract the new-critical and deconstructive concentration exclusively on the text. It restores context, and it often entangles with reader-response criticism—with the historical ambition to appreciate how texts are read when published. Even the most cleverly conceptualized and operationalized of inquiries, then, must reckon with the rhetorical conditions of their technical terms—which can be useful only if connected intelligibly to their antecedents and implications. Whether imaginative or historical, tropal or narratival, this intelligibility is a must.

Furthermore social scientists need to rethink the notion that they can stipulate new or narrowed meanings for technical terms, in order to cast off earlier meanings as though they were old baggage or clothes to be discarded once and for all. As J.L. Austin wrote, "A word never—well, hardly ever—shakes off its etymology and its formation. In spite of all changes in and extensions of and additions to its meanings, and indeed rather pervading and governing them, there will persist the old idea."[11] The fine philosopher-poet of ordinary language and mundane history for the communities of our times has been Stanley Cavell.[12]

No doubt this is easier for most late-modern scholars to accept for historical than for imaginative, poetic etymologies. But it is true for both, and in much the same way. In fact, the two kinds of etymology often serve substantive arguments in precisely the same way. In telling rhetorical terms, they are primarily devices of invention, meaning that etymologies of both kinds project structures of inference and argument.

Please note, though, that figures of invention must not be reduced to heuristics in some objectivist sense. They are not mere devices of discovery which contribute no evidence toward justifying the resulting claims. (This parallels the positivist contrast between contexts of discovery and contexts of justification, another dichotomy which we have good reasons to reject.)[13] On the contrary, tropes of invention become intrinsic to the evidence and reasons for whatever the positions argued. Moreover, this is precisely what imaginative etymologies often do for good arguments in the humanities, the social sciences, and politics.

Presented as derivations capable of summary in a sentence or two, imaginative etymologies comprise a kind of evidence. Higher-and-harder-than-thou critics are perfectly prepared, of course, to agree that most arguments in the social sciences—let alone the humanities—are soft and confused. The critics sneer that many social scientists substitute silly word games of one kind or another for the proper proofs and solid evidence of true Science. Perhaps the most provocative thing about the thesis, therefore, is its insistence that imaginative etymology often is good evidence, even in the highest and hardest of the social sciences.

Evidence as an Example

A pedagogical example of imaginative etymology as evidence might be a treatment of evidence itself. Social scientists generally talk as though evidence were mere data, simply a set of facts. Once, I wanted some students to understand instead how evidence is information arranged persuasively within an argument. The resulting discussion pushes at the limits of imaginative etymology, since it plays on unrelated etymologies of three or four words rather than one. Etymologically, please notice, *evidence* is *e-vidence*, from *evidere* in Latin. As the *Oxford English Dictionary* says, *evidence* is an *out-seeing*, a *seeing out*—that is, a *making to appear*. (The German *aussehen* works much the same way.) Thus, the *OED* begins its inventory of meanings:

> I. To be in evidence, to be present.
> 1. The quality or condition of being evident; clearness, evidentness; *in evidence:* actually present; prominent, conspicuous.
> 2. Manifestation; display (obsolete).
>
> II. That which manifests or makes evident.
> 3. An appearance from which inferences may be drawn; an indication, mark, sign, token, trace.
> 4. Examples, instance.
> 5. Ground for belief, testimony or facts tending to prove or disprove any conclusion.
>
> III. Legal uses of 5.
> 6. Information, whether in the form of personal testimony, the language, of documents, or the production of material objects, that is given in a legal investigation, to establish the fact or point in question.

So far we have something on the order of historical etymology, and we can note from the *OED* that the English word arises in the Reformation and changes in the eighteenth century (with Lord Shaftesbury) to a more specifically scientific usage.

This illuminates the status of evidence in postmodern sciences, because it encourages us to focus on rhetorical questions of audience and setting: making to appear to whom, where, when, and so forth. Already we are reaching beyond historical into imaginative etymology, but this is where the real fun begins! Next we can remember that, by Nietzschean and Heideggerian etymology, which always seems poetic and imaginative to me, *myth* means much the same: a *making present*, a *making to appear*. Since we see already that myths are symbolic stories that present whole accounts of events,[14] we can recognize that evidence works in similar ways—not as isolated facts but as parts of persuasive accounts.

Moreover, we can notice a nominal resemblance of *evidence* to *events* and *evince*. Late-modern sciences often seek to endow evidence with the ethos of the events themselves speaking, so that we can simply hear and see the facts of any matter adequately evidenced. This is exactly the province of evincing: just as we say that the professor evinces a fine knowledge of physics, we may say that the historical evidence evinces a compelling case for some hypothesis about pricing or party realignment.

Evince comes from *ex vincere*, literally *out of* or *from conquering*. *Conviction* has the same root, so that it suggests *conquering-with*. By contrast, rhetorical *persuasion* stems from *suadere*, with an unmistakable implication of *sweetening*. The point from imaginative etymology, as you can anticipate, is that late-modern sciences treat evidence as something that is to conquer us. Evincing, too, means to make manifest, to show plainly, compellingly. "Though it has lost its original English meaning of conquering, it now means 'to show beyond a doubt' and, in that sense, some trace of conquering remains."[15] Then the argument from imaginative etymology becomes that we should return evidence to its mythic sense of presentation and its rhetorical sense of persuasion, turning away from its latter-day confusion with evincing. Rather than conquering by sheer data, evidence should mean our seeing-out of information and our making-of-it-to-appear (in arguments) to others or even to ourselves.

Information as an Instance

A related example of imaginative etymology as good evidence is the very notion of information just invoked. Thanks to cybernetics and cognitive science, we are beginning to reassess the late-modern sense of *information*. From the origins of the information revolution, a century or more ago, people have worked to regard information as raw content that is capable of representation in diverse forms with no alteration in substance or meaning. Thus, the language of media came to dominate our talk about information: senders, messages, channels, receivers, and so forth. Oddly the information was the unformed data, to be conveyed with minimum distortion from one place or person to another. Once collected and communicated, the information could be analyzed in various ways to ascertain its significance. But the information was separate from its form and its significance.

This perspective permitted immense leaps in our technologies of information and communication. It also taught us about its limitations. We learned that there can be no information without communication or mediation, because information is intrinsically a sharing of sorts. (Of course, that is why evidence should be seen as a communal construction with arguments rather than a conquering imposition of given facts.) Yet we learned also that there can be no communication without what has been regarded as "distortion," because such sharing must span differences by coordinating rather than negating them. For a long time, we regarded such "distortion" narrowly, as a mere loss of information. But of late, we are coming to reassess it in broader terms as "translation," implying a possible enrichment of information. No longer is information raw data or mere content; rather it is the stylized content that emerges from us and enters into us, forming us from without and within.

Accordingly, we are learning that there is no communication without analysis of information. To convey or transmit information from sender to receiver, we must analyze the information sent according to the very characteristics that make the receiver different from the sender. And this implies that there can be no analysis of information without some concern for its meaning or significance. Therefore, the earlier ideal of unanalyzed or unformed information—the notion of data fully separable from their forms of communication—yields to a sense of information as content both formed and forming. From the artificial intelligence work in the two Cambridges to the computer innovations in California and Japan, we are starting to appreciate how *information* is in-formed and in-forming. Marshall McLuhan, the Media Lab, and many others have come in diverse ways to much the same insight: media are not wholly external to messages; instead each interpenetrates the other.[16] Thus form is in in-form-ation, intrinsic to it, and we are formed through and through by the information that enters into us to structure our awareness and action. I find little in the historical etymology of information to warrant this imaginative reading, but there is much in our practices and problems of information to recommend it. The poetic etymology is more insightful and even persuasive about our politics and histories.

Imaginative etymology succeeds as evidence when it contributes to persuasive arrays of information. As evidence, imaginative etymology not only adds (content) to our information but (re)forms, (re)orders what we knew already. Now, due to this additional information, we must know differently—and we must hope to know better—than before.

Neologisms as Illustrations

This even happens at another frontier of imaginative etymology: when it becomes the intentional invention of etymology for a new word. The social sciences have yet to equal the formal and natural sciences in this endeavor, but interesting examples do arise from time to time. A personal favorite is the meditation by Raymond Williams on implications of "distant seeing" in the word manufactured complete with etymology to name that central implement of late-modern cultures, *television*.[17]

Another case is William Riker's clever etymological justification for coining the awkward word *heresthetics*, in order to avoid association with what ought to be termed *rhetorics*.[18] Riker's understandable fear seems to have been that his implicit apostasy in turning from the Hard Science of rational choice, which he helped to found, to the Soft Art of rhetoric could devastate his credibility among political scientists.[19] So he labored mightily to generate an etymology for the construction of heresthetics—to show how it is behavioral rather than persuasive, a matter of lasting structure rather than ephemeral speech. Gainsaid by his own examples, the invented etymology became Riker's main (if to me unpersuasive) evidence for heresthetics as separate from rhetorics. His gambit seems to be succeeding, yet some of the game theorists now edging into "heresthetics" are able to recognize their efforts as rhetorics.

Other invented etymologies serve the inventors even better. Easy examples are Sigmund Freud's poetic etymology stipulated for the *id* and the one Hannah Arendt provided for *totalitarianism*.[20] Such efforts hint that, to succeed as evidence, any etymology—imaginative or historical—must make persuasive ties throughout a field of information. It must fit rather than contradict the rest of a text; it must configure rather than cross-cut the pattern of an archive; it must connect rather than disrupt the entries in a database.

Meaning Variance as Proception

A persuasive play of meanings closely akin (if not identical) to imaginative etymology can even operate prospectively, reaching toward future conditions. Thus, new senses of terms can project whole theories and cultures to articulate and support them. Hayden White calls this a "prefiguration of the phenomenal field."[21] I like to talk about future-oriented *proception* by comparison with *perception* in the present and *conception* devoted to explaining the past.[22] Refiguring an important word to give it different poetics, including invented etymologies, has become an important device of inquiry and persuasion within the natural sciences and history, as well as the social sciences.

The twentieth century's semantic scandals of the natural sciences furnish instructive cases in point.[23] From Fleck, Kuhn, and Feyerabend onward, historically minded philosophers of science have emphasized how meanings of key terms vary from one theory or paradigm to the next.[24] Mass does not mean the same for Einstein as for Newton, as the single most famous example has it. Nor, of course, does force or gravity or light or most other key concepts of modern physics. The lesson here is a simple corollary of the structuralist principle that words can mean only in systems and not as isolated designators. Einstein's physical concepts differ radically from Newton's, and quantum principles further alter the meanings of key terms in physics. A theory as a whole defines its key terms. When a scientific community switches from one theory to another, while keeping many names and labels for its concepts intact, then their meanings and the implicated etymologies vary—sometimes immensely. Since the shifted meanings are importantly different, their etymologies are apt to be invented and imaginative, even where the new theory is not relying on neologisms.

During the transitions from dominance by one theory to hegemony by another, moreover, the upstart relies crucially on its evocative, poetic projection of vaguely defined possibilities in order to persuade people to pursue its vision of reality. In conventional, empiricist terms, it could not yet enjoy enough testing and refinement to be evidenced better than its previously established competitor. Thus, Feyerabend shows for Galileo's revolutionary physics how his changes in the meanings of key terms (as well as some pretty "creative" experimentation) could attract adherents long before there had been adequate opportunities to develop the new meanings into conventionally verified views.[25]

The figure of giving new meanings to old terms is *catachresis*.[26] Historiographical arguments can do this through imaginative etymologies. Telling examples are easy to spot in historical accounts of revolutions. When liberal historians want to treat the French Revolution as a radical break with medieval institutions, they are apt to construe *revolution* as a turning back against established ways.[27] Often these scholars tend to deny that "the American Revolution" was worthy of the name, arguing that it kept too much of the prior regime intact. When republican historians portray the American Revolution as fundamental for later politics, they move to etymologize *revolution* as a re-turn to founding or constitutional principles, with events re-volving like a record on a turntable.[28] Even in historiography, of course, the stakes often concern present or future actions that might follow from one account versus another. Catachretic etymologies accordingly can persuade by proceiving events yet to come.

NOT JUST DATA BUT REALITY

> Of course the issues [of culture and society] could not all be understood simply by analysis of the words. On the contrary, most . . . persisted within and beyond the linguistic analysis. Yet many of these issues, I found, could not really be thought through, and some of them, I believe, cannot even be focused unless we are conscious of the words as elements of the problems.
>
> —Raymond Williams

Because it works best as evidence when it makes myriad connections to other evidence, imaginative etymology readily becomes as well a trope of argument.[28] Like models and statistics in the social sciences, the argumentative trope of imaginative etymology pre- or con-figures whole logics of persuasion. Historical etymology can work in the same way.

A humanities example is Marlena Corcoran's philological argument about Immanuel Kant's *Critique of Judgment*.[30] Kant's German word for judgment is *Urteilskraft*. Corcoran explains that *Teil* is *part*; but whereas *Ur* is *originary* in some contexts, here it combines with *Teil* to form *Urteil* as dealing and dividing into parts. Indeed *einteilen* means to divide or categorize. Corcoran observes that Kant's movement is from lower parts to higher, as in the Roman law he knew so well. This sets up a striking contrast between such dealing or dividing and Kant's word for reason, *Vernunft*, which means *grasping*. Thus, when Kant suggests that our aesthetic judgment proceeds through application of the "law of specification" to nature, he follows the logic and language of Roman law. The harmony between nature and the judging subject asserted by Kant as a "fortunate coincidence" seems redolent to Corcoran of the "Fortunate Fall" for Christians, and so Kant's subject has (even is?) a divine and mystical heart of irrationality coordinated in judgment with nature.

Here the point is less Corcoran's virtuosity of reading than her way of configuring a major problematic of Kant's *Critique*. She provides many persuasive connections between the specifics of her etymologies and the diverse details of the text. (The paper offers a profusion of ties beyond those summarized here.) Assuming that Corcoran is right (as a matter of history in word meanings) to set aside the originary sense of *Ur*, then we could readily imagine enriching her reading still further by turning it into avowedly imaginative etymology. We could invoke the originary sense of *Ur* (as in *Urmyth*) to configure a coordinated set of connections between the node of dividing versus grasping and the node of the Fortunate Fall from Grace in the Garden of Eden. Then we might comprehend still better Kant's (and Heidegger's Kantian) arguments about (aesthetic) judgment as the origin of human attunement to the world.

At this point, though, the game gets bigger than single arguments or particular texts. How the issues grow becomes evident when we turn to Raymond Williams and his "vocabulary of key words." Corcoran shows how any etymological evidence depends on connections throughout texts or arguments, with each connection a confirmation of sorts. These ties pattern our reading of the whole text. Likewise they offer standards and procedures for the whole of an argument, working in the same manner as models or statistics to provide and validate the overall shape or figure of the argument. That is why they are *tropes of argument*—in much the same sense that metaphors, oxymorons, and hyperboles are tropes (or figures) of speech. The tropal arguments of one era are the literal or positive or historical arguments of another period. And likewise the historical arguments of one time are the poetic or mythic or imaginative figures that inform another epoch.

What the Williams book on *Key Words* shows is how etymologies may configure substantive arguments about events, societies, institutions, and the other issues addressed by various of the human sciences. The Williams etymologies for key words explicate ties among structural and operational details throughout late-modern societies. Defining *culture*, *myth*, *representation*, *society*, and other important concepts, Williams coordinated manifold data, information, instances, specifics, stories, theories, and other elements of argument about those societies. The results are patterns of telling detail, figured as etymological evidence and configuring his arguments as etymological. Williams advanced these patterns as abductive figures of inference about his (largely Marxian) issues concerning modern civilization. Each etymology evokes scores of ties to familiar phenomena in modern societies, and together the set of etymologies provides an exceptionally persuasive argument for a set of positions that usually leave me, at least, in some disagreement. Much the same thing, though with less explicit attention to etymology, is accomplished by William Connolly in his analysis of several "essentially contested concepts" as *The Terms of Political Discourse*.[31]

Because the Williams and Connolly coordinations of meanings with etymologies are feats of political theory, and thus imagination, their books underscore a crucial lesson: *All extensive etymologies must be imaginative.* In addition, they suggest that one practical standard for what to count as "extensive" is whether an etymology pursues issues beyond the histories of words considered mostly as ends in themselves. Albeit in historical and humanistic veins, the Williams and Connolly tomes illustrate how etymologies can achieve larger ambitions. This is the same set of lessons long ago suggested by Giambattista Vico, and his work merits rereading in this context.[32] Yet it is equally a set of lessons as recent as today's news analysis, as Lawrence Weschler has demonstrated in his imaginative-etymology-as-political-history of the Solidarity movement in Poland.[33]

We can recognize imaginative etymology in past arguments that remain famous and influential. An obvious political example is how Thomas Hobbes invoked imaginative etymology to braid together several reasons for complete obedience to the Sovereign. Hobbes maintained that the Sovereign's *author-ity* to command obedience derives from the meaning of *author-izing* as *author-ing*. The subjects, or so claimed Hobbes, have authored the Sovereign—thus *author-izing* its acts. This means that the subjects are the ultimate authors of the Sovereign's acts, which is to say that the Sovereign's acts are deeds of the subjects themselves. Therefore the subjects can disobey the acts of the Sovereign only by disobeying themselves. Such self-contradiction is a morally obnoxious and impermissible move, concluded Hobbes. The lesson is not that this conceptual dance is debatable in logic and in history, as surely it is. Rather we can learn from this instance that (1) Hobbes presented his case for absolute obedience through an etymology invented to tell the meaning of *authority*, and (2) his etymology aptly configures an argument plausible within his larger theories of political power and obligation.

The Center Cannot Hold

> Concepts, like individuals, have their histories and are just as incapable of withstanding the ravages of time as are individuals. But in and through all this they retain a kind of homesickness for the scenes of their childhood.
>
> —Soren Kierkegaard

Imaginative etymology is especially prominent these days in the social and political criticism produced by deconstructivists. Their deconstructions often show how apparent meaning and evidence could be contradicted by etymological meaning and evidence, as generated through historical research *or* imaginative connection. A skillful example is Michael J. Shapiro's etymological deconstruction of sociological and political arguments by James Q. Wilson about criminal investigation and punishment.[34] Enlarging imaginatively on the historical etymology of *tasks* as *taxings* (from *taxo* and *taxare* in Latin) as *fixed payments to a king or feudal superior*, Shapiro argues that Wilson's avowed program of replacing top-down administration fails due to its thorough implication in contrary figures—not only of speech, but especially of argument.

Shapiro is a political deconstructivist with a negative, mostly Foucauldian mission to scoff at hierarchy and sneer at domination. In some cases, however, the deconstructive moment can lead into something of a reconstruction—which also becomes configured by etymology. A particularly apt example is William Corlett's book on *Community Without Unity*.[35] By evidence and figures of etymology, some historical and most imaginative, he first disassembles the principles of political community advanced by many moderns, revealing immense troubles of evidence and reasoning within recent texts. Some followers of Foucault evoke textual and cultural contradictions as objects for snickering. This is because they can imagine no reprieve from our dilemmas of domination. Many of the neo-Marxists, such as Williams, explicate contradictions to give hope that our structures of domination must collapse of their own dynamics. But Corlett writes more in the style of Derrida than Foucault or Marx. Accordingly he turns out to be less interested in social or textual contradictions as such. He emphasizes political ironies, oxymorons, aporias, and the other poetic figures of incongruity, dispersion, and extravagance. These he traces in various texts and practices. Having done such deconstruction, he then joins it to the historical etymology of *community* as *com-munare* or *with-giving*—that is, *giving-together*. He ends with imaginative ties of etymology to such Derridean dynamics as *the supplement* and *extravagance*. The result is a playful and persuasive case for reading overtly contrary theories and practices of community to support his Derridean ideals more than their own professed principles.

Were this a book in itself, rather than one among several chapters about poetic history, I would be tempted to argue that the current turn to literary and political deconstruction arises in important part from our growing awareness that evidence and reasoning cannot stay bifurcated into synthetic and analytic compartments. To me, this is a major lesson of Jacques Derrida's strictures against Western, logicist penchants for dichotomies and dualisms.[36]

More adventurously still, I would explain that such arguments take some of their main justifications from imaginative etymologies. Indeed, a proclivity for this kind of argument distinguishes a whole family of dissenters from the Western project of controlling and dominating nature through skillful representation of it.[37] The shared technique is to repoeticize our languages, our arguments, our worlds. A host of aphorisms testify to this imaginatively etymological approach; browsing just a few pages in the *Oxford Book of Aphorisms* suffices to suggest that this ambition is an enduring legacy of the last couple of centuries, as we have moved into high- and late-modern times:

> *Ralph Waldo Emerson*: "All Language is fossil poetry."
>
> *Georg Christoph Lichtenberg*: "Most of our expressions are metaphorical—the philosophy of our forefathers lies hidden in them."
>
> *Charles Baudelaire*: "The immense profundity of thought contained in commonplace turns of phrase—holes burrowed by generations of ants."
>
> *Thomas Carlyle*: "The coldest word was once a glowing new metaphor."[38]

Thus the rationales and tactics of genealogy in Nietzsche, Foucault, and others depend more than a little on the persuasive power of etymologies, imaginative even more than historical.

At this level, imaginative etymology leads into what Paul Hernadi and Katherine Hayles call the "erotics of argumentation."[39] As a prime topic in the rhetoric of evidence, this explores how our dispositions of desire inform our senses of the adequacy of arguments. Thus, imaginative etymologies play on and to our aesthetics of image, rhythm, voice, and resonance. These tie more readily to our senses of myth and poetry than our ideas of history or science. Yet no efforts, modern or otherwise, can eliminate these tropes of argument and aesthetics of desire from our histories and sciences of society. Nor does our ignoring their dynamics improve the arguments of us human scientists. One value of imaginative etymology is to turn such ignorance, embarrassment, and outrage into positive but playful modes of study. Thus a little imagination suffices to turn Michael Walzer's ruminations on the origins of citizenship into an inventive rhetoric of citizenship that configures and defends policy positions on current issues through etymological appeals.[40] Or in a different vein, the tropal imagination of Hayden White can turn the cultural etymology of Michel Foucault toward a better sense of the dynamics of social inquiry.[41]

The Play's the Thing

> As men abound in copiousness of language, so they become more wise, or more mad, than ordinary.
>
> —Thomas Hobbes

For us, the most important thing to stress about imaginative etymology is its insistence on *poetic play*. As an exploration of the powers of words, etymological evidence and argument require a keen sense of the inter*play* of meanings and connections. They seek to dis*play* our spheres of activity as languages, as vocabularies, as myths, as fields of terminology and mutual implication. Especially they encourage us to *play* with the aesthetic possibilities of our information, particularly as we configure it into inferences and it configures us into characters in the ongoing *plays* of our lives.

Through this emphasis on play, we can recognize that imaginative etymology may take several forms, many of them evident in the examples already provided. These forms also may be regarded as distinct dynamics or strategies of any etymology with an imaginative twist:

A. Play poetically with the components of a word—as in *community* and *re-presentation* (Pitkin and Redner).[42]

B. Play poetically with the implicitly etymological, tropal, or historical configurations of argument—as in logical, psychological, and social *con-straints* suggesting webs of belief or networks of meaning rather than fully axiomatic systems or merely causal links (see the treatment of Philip Converse that follows).

C. Play poetically with mistaken deconstructions—as in *comm-unity* and *iron-y* (see the earlier discussion of Corlett).

D. Play poetically with historical contexts—so that *citizenship* (not a Greek but a Roman concept, partly republican and partly imperial) fits mass republics better than participatory democracies; or so that *revolutions* as *re-volvings* have an aspiration to recover or return to past conditions (see the discussions of Arendt and Williams).[43]

E. Play poetically with other forms of the root—for example, *rationality* as *rationing* to understand economistic conceptions of reason and choice; or *authority* as *author-ing* as *author-izing* (Hobbes); or *authority* as *augmentation* as *tradition* (Arendt) and therefore as *nurturance* (Richard Sennett).[44]

F. Play poetically with nominally similar words that have different roots—*evidence* and *evince*, for example, or reasoned judgment as grasping (*Vernunft*) and reasoned justment as dividing (Corcoran on *Urteilskraft*).

Sometimes imaginative etymology might be confused with the persuasive definition and persuasive naming well known to the social sciences, as in the notorious "statistical tests of significance," which routinely get mistaken by social scientists (let alone others) for guarantors of substantive significance when they only concern inferential properties of different sample sizes.[45] But the playful dynamics of imaginative etymology move in opposite directions, seeking to display the erotics and aesthetics of argumentation rather than to exploit them covertly.

Playful exploration of meaning connections can enable imaginative etymology to improve our understanding of work throughout the historical arts and sciences. Such connections can surface, for example, in our parsing of arguments among the political scientists who study elections. These scholars depend for evidence on configuring elections as events of *voting* and *representation*. Their terms get etymologized historically and imaginatively as *voicing* and *re-presentation*, despite findings that insistently question whether elections do—or even could—fulfill mandates of voicing and re-presentation. Much the same emphasis on re-presentation also holds for the economists who study agency theories of rational choice in corporations and for the epistemologists who pose modelling accounts of the knowledge generated by various sciences.

The main reason to become more conscious of our reliance on such connections is to make them and evaluate them better. Within the social sciences, a good case in point is the pioneering work by Philip Converse on political ideologies as mass belief systems.[46] Unaware of the subtle ties of meaning encouraged by imaginative etymology, Converse portrayed belief systems as constrained logically, psychologically, or socially. For all of its difficulties, Converse's argument continues to exert immense influence on political psychology and public-opinion research. Current interest in modelling beliefs in n-dimensional space makes sense mainly in terms of the Converse assumptions.

The key trouble with the Converse scheme, many critics agree, is its inability to comprehend how belief systems change step by step—that is, how people learn. This trouble remains with the n-dimensional mapping of beliefs, because it includes no substantive conception of the connections among beliefs that would enable us to trace how changes in a belief should and do induce changes in others. A good solution to that problem, though, lies in Converse's own figure of constraint. This word projects powerful etymological echoes of drawing together, as in the straining-with-one-another of strands in a web. Visualizing beliefs as nodes in a network lets changing tensions among the strands explain how changes in one node become communicated in specific ways to other nodes. It even encourages us to understand how the nodes or beliefs themselves are intersections of the connecting strands (of experience or thought), rather than a separate kind of entity. This permits us to eliminate the perplexing (modernist) dichotomy that continues to bedevil accounts of belief systems: a strange contrast between the many different nodes of content (the synthetic beliefs) and the formal connection of those nodes into a single system through a small set of logical ties (the analytic operators such as *and*, *or*, *unless*, and *implies*). It also helps us to overcome the unworkable barrier against inferential ties between the two main kinds of beliefs quarantined by modernists: facts and values.

We get all this through a little poetry of sorts. Indeed I would argue that the imagery of cognitive networks or webs of belief implicit in the Converse talk of constraint explains why his early work persuaded so many of his colleagues. If so, a telling irony is how such network notions have come to the fore in supplanting some of the conclusions and methodology generated by Converse and *n*-dimensional modellers.[47] These are the substantive kinds of contributions awaiting the human scientists who pursue imaginative etymology as a type of evidence and a trope of argument. The same goes for other resources in the rhetoric and history of inquiry when pursued as intrinsic aspects of any human science.

Notes

1. See John S. Nelson, *Ironic Politics*, unpublished Ph.D. dissertation, University of North Carolina Department of Political Science, Chapel Hill, N.C., 1977.

2. See Ursula K. Le Guin, *The Dispossessed* (New York: Harper and Row, 1974); J. Roland Pennock and John W. Chapman, eds., *Nomos XXI: Compromise in Ethics, Law, and Politics* (New York: New York University Press, 1979).

3. Works that make this (imaginative) etymological move are legion. See Carl J. Friedrich, ed., *Nomos II: Community* (New York: Atherton Press, 1959); Fred R. Dallmayr, ed., *From Contract to Community* (New York: Marcel Dekker, 1978); Glenn Tinder, *Community* (Baton Rouge, Louisiana State University Press, 1980).

4. See D.N. McCloskey: *The Rhetoric of Economics* (Madison: University of Wisconsin Press, 1985), especially 54–68; *If You're So Smart* (Chicago: University of Chicago Press, 1990); *Knowledge and Persuasion in Economics* (New York: Cambridge University Press, 1994).

5. See Arjo Klamer, D.N. McCloskey, and Robert W. Solow, eds., *The Consequences of Economic Rhetoric* (New York: Cambridge University Press, 1988); Marianne A. Ferber and Julie A. Nelson, *Beyond Economic Man* (Chicago: University of Chicago Press, 1993).

6. See Ludwig Wittgenstein, *Philosophical Investigations*, G. E. M. Anscombe, trans. (New York: Macmillan, third edition, 1958); W. V. O. Quine, *Word and Object* (Cambridge: MIT Press, 1960).

7. See Jonathan Culler, *Structuralist Poetics* (Ithaca: Cornell University Press, 1975).

8. In my home field of political theory, see Quentin Skinner: "Meaning and Understanding in the History of Ideas," *History and Theory* 8, 1 (1969): 3–53; "Conventions and the Understanding of Speech Acts," *Philosophical Quarterly* 21, 2 (April 1970): 113–138; "'Social Meaning' and the Explanation of Social Actions," in *Philosophy, Politics, and Society (Fourth Series)*, ed. Peter Laslett and W. G. Runciman (Oxford: Basil Blackwell, 1972), 136–157; "Some Problems in the Analysis of Political Thought and Action," *Political Theory* 2, 3 (August 1974): 277–303. Also see J. G. A. Pocock, *Politics, Language, and Time* (New York: Atheneum, 1972).

9. For the new history of political theory, See J. G. A. Pocock, *The Ancient Constitution and the Feudal Law* (New York: Norton, 1967); J. G. A. Pocock, *The Machiavellian Moment* (Princeton: Princeton University Press, 1975); Quentin Skinner, *The Foundations of Modern Political Thought* (Cambridge: Cambridge University Press, in two volumes, 1978); John Dunn, *The Political Thought of John Locke* (Cambridge: Cambridge University Press, 1969); John Dunn, *Political Obligation in Its Historical Context* (Cambridge: Cambridge University Press, 1980); Richard Ashcraft, *Revolutionary Politics and Locke's TWO TREATISES OF GOVERNMENT* (Princeton: Princeton University Press, 1986); Terence Ball, *Reappraising Political Theory* (Oxford: Oxford University Press, 1995). The new-historical emphasis on Locke, the American founders, and what Pocock calls "the Atlantic Republican tradition" arises from appreciating specifically political intelligence (within popular contexts of history) on the part of works often called "political philosophy" but easily condemned as incoherent philosophically. These have a poetic, political power that modernist, analytical philosophy cannot parse.

10. See Thomas L. Dumm, *Democracy and Punishment* (Madison: University of Wisconsin Press, 1987); Stephen A. Tyler, *The Unspeakable* (Madison: University of Wisconsin Press, 1987).

11. J.L. Austin, "A Plea for Excuses," *Philosophical Papers*, 1961.

12. See Stanley Cavell: *Must We Mean What We Say?* (Cambridge: Cambridge University Press, 1976); *The Claim of Reason* (New York: Oxford University Press, 1979); *Themes Out of School* (Chicago: University of Chicago Press, 1984); *In Quest of the Ordinary* (Chicago: University of Chicago Press, 1988); *This New Yet Unapproachable America* (Albuquerque, N.M.: Living Batch Press, 1989); *Conditions Handsome and Unhandsome* (Chicago: University of Chicago Press, 1990); *A Pitch of Philosophy* (Cambridge: Harvard University Press, 1994); *Philosophical Passages* (Cambridge: Blackwell, 1995). Also see John Hollander, "Stanley Cavell and The Claim of Reason," *Critical Inquiry* 6, 4 (Summer 1980): 575–588; Michael Fischer, *Stanley Cavell and Literary Skepticism* (Chicago: University of Chicago Press, 1989); Richard Fleming and Michael Payne, eds., *The Senses of Stanley Cavell* (Lewisburg, Pa.: Bucknell University Press, 1989).

13. See Norwood Russell Hanson, *Patterns of Discovery* (New York: Cambridge University Press, 1965).

14. See John S. Nelson, "Political Mythmaking for Post-Moderns," in *Spheres of Argument*, ed. Bruce E. Gronbeck (Annandale, Va.: Speech Communication Association, 1989), 175–183.

15. William and Mary Morris, *Dictionary of Word and Phrase Origins* (New York: Harper and Row, second edition, 1977).

16. See Marshall McLuhan, *Understanding Media* (New York: McGraw-Hill, 1964); Stewart Brand, *The Media Lab* (New York: Viking Press, 1987).

17. See Raymond Williams, "Distance," in *Raymond Williams on Television*, ed. Alan O'Connor (London: Routledge, 1989), 13–21.

18. See William H. Riker, "Preface," in *The Art of Political Manipulation* (New Haven: Yale University Press, 1986), ix–xi.

19. See William H. Riker: "Political Theory and the Art of Heresthetics," in *Political Science*, ed. Ada W. Finifter (Washington, D.C.: American Political Science Association, 1983), 47–67; "The Heresthetics of Constitution-Making," *American Political Science Review* 78, 1 (March 1984), 1–16.

20. See Sigmund Freud: *The Ego and the Id*, trans. Joan Riviere, ed. James Strachey (New York: Norton, 1960); *Beyond the Pleasure Principle*, trans. and ed. James Strachey (New York: Norton, 1961). Also see Hannah Arent, *The Origins of Totalitarianism* (New York: Harcourt Brace Jovanovich, (1951), fourth and complete edition, 1973).

21. See Hayden White, *Metahistory* (Baltimore: Johns Hopkins University Press, 1973).

22. See Nelson, "Political Mythmaking for Post-Moderns."

23. See Michael Martin, "Referential Variance and Scientific Objectivity," *British Journal for the Philosophy of Science* 22, 1 (March 1971): 17–26; Earl R. MacCormac, "Meaning Variance and Metaphor," *British Journal for the Phi-*

losophy of Science 22, 2 (June 1971): 145–159; J.N. Hattiangadi, "Alternatives and Incommensurables: The Case of Darwin and Kelvin," *Philosophy of Science* 38, 4 (December 1971): 502–507; Derek L. Phillips, "Paradigms and Incommensurability," *Theory and Society* 2, 1 (Spring 1975): 37–61.

24. See Ludwik Fleck, *Genesis and Development of a Scientific Fact*, ed. Thaddeus J. Trenn and Robert K. Merton, trans. Fred Bradley and Thaddeus J. Trenn (Chicago: University of Chicago Press [1935], 1979). Also see Thomas S. Kuhn: *The Structure of Scientific Revolutions* (Chicago: University of Chicago Press [1962], enlarged edition, 1970); *The Essential Tension* (Chicago: University of Chicago Press, 1977). And see Paul K. Feyerabend, *Against Method* (Atlantic Highlands, N.J.: Humanities Press, 1975); Paul K. Feyerabend, *Science in a Free Society* (London: New Left Books, 1978).

25. See Feyerabend, *Against Method*, 69–161.

26. See Richard A. Lanham, *A Handlist of Rhetorical Terms* (Berkeley: University of California Press [1968], second edition, 1991), 31.

27. See Charles Tilly: *From Mobilization to Revolution* (Reading, Mass.: Addison-Wesley, 1978); *The Contentious French* (Cambridge: Harvard University Press, 1986); *European Revolutions* (Oxford: Basil Blackwell, 1993). Compare the *Oxford English Dictionary* on revolve and revolution.

28. See Hannah Arendt, *On Revolution* (New York: Viking Press, 1963). Also see John S. Nelson, "Political Foundations for Rhetoric of Inquiry," in *The Rhetorical Turn*, ed. Herbert W. Simon (Chicago: University of Chicago Press, 1990), 258–289.

29. See John S. Nelson, "Models, Statistics, and Other Tropes of Politics: Or, Whatever Happened to Argumentation in Political Science," in *Argument in Transition*, ed. David Zarefsky, Malcolm O. Sillars, and Jack Rhodes (Annandale, Va.: Speech Communication Association, 1983), 213–229.

30. See Marlena Corcoran, "The Nature of the Subject," Symposium on Kant 200, Project on Rhetoric of Inquiry, Iowa City, 1990.

31. See William E. Connolly, *The Terms of Political Discourse* (Lexington, Mass.: D.C. Heath, 1974).

32. See Giambattista Vico: *The New Science of Giambattista Vico*, trans. Thomas Goddard Bergin and Max Harold Fisch (Ithaca: Cornell University Press, unabridged translation of the third edition [1744], 1976); *On the Study Methods of Our Time*, trans. Elio Gianturco (Indianapolis: Bobbs-Merrill [1709], 1965).

33. See Lawrence Weschler, *The Passion of Poland* (New York: Pantheon Books, 1984).

34. See Michael J. Shapiro, "The Rhetoric of Social Science: The Political Responsibilities of the Scholar," in *The Rhetoric of the Human Sciences*, ed. John S. Nelson, Allan Megill, and D.N. McCloskey (Madison: University of Wisconsin Press, 1987), 363–380, especially 370–375.

35. See William Corlett, *Community Without Unity* (Durham: Duke University Press, 1989).

36. See Jacques Derrida: *Writing and Difference*, trans. Alan Bass (Chicago: University of Chicago Press [1967], 1978); *Dissemination*, trans. Barbara Johnson (Chicago: University of Chicago Press [1972], 1981); *Positions*, trans. Alan Bass (Chicago: University of Chicago Press [1972], 1981).

37. See John S. Nelson, "Political Theory as Political Rhetoric," in *What Should Political Theory Be Now?* ed. Nelson (Albany: State University of New York Press, 1983), 169–240.

38. John Gross, ed., *The Oxford Book of Aphorisms* (Oxford: Oxford University Press, 1983), 280–284.

39. See Paul Hernadi, "The Erotics of Retrospection: Historytelling, Audience Response, and the Strategies of Desire," *New Literary History* 12, 2 (Winter 1981): 243–252; N. Katherine Hayles, "Eroticism in Language, or Argument Is Not All," Symposium on the Rhetoric of the Disciplines: Next Steps, Project on Rhetoric of Inquiry, Iowa City, 1988.

40. See Michael Walzer, *Obligations* (Cambridge: Harvard University Press, 1970); John S. Nelson, "Tropes of Political Argument in America: Toward Mythics Modes of Rhetorical Analysis," in *Argument in Controversy*, ed. Donn W. Parson (Annandale, Va: Speech Communication Association, 1991), 73–79.

41. See Hayden White: *Metahistory*; *Tropics of Discourse* (Baltimore: Johns Hopkins University, 1987), especially 230–260. Also see John S. Nelson, "Tropal History and the Social Sciences," *History and Theory* 19, 4 (1980): 80–101.

42. See Hanna Fenichel Pitkin: *The Concept of Representation* (Berkeley: University of California Press, 1967); (Berkeley: University of California Press, 1972). Also see Harry Redner, "Representation and the Crisis of Post-Modernism," *PS* 20, 3 (Summer 1987): 673–679.

43. See Williams, *Key Words*; Arendt, *On Revolution*.

44. See Hannah Arendt, "Tradition and the Modern Age," *Between Past and Future* (New York: Viking Press [1963], enlarged edition, 1968), 17–40; Richard Sennett, *Authority* (New York: Knopf, 1980).

45. See Philip L. Bearsley, "Substantive Significance vs. Quantitative Rigor in Political Inquiry: Are the Two Compatible?" *International Interactions* 1, 1 (1984): 27–40; D.N. McCloskey, "Why Economic Historians Should Stop Relying on Statistical Tests of Significance, and Lead Economists and Historians into the Promised Land," *Newsletter of the Cliometrics Society* 2, 2 (December 1986): 5–7; McCloskey, "The Rhetoric of Significance Tests," in *The Rhetoric of Economics*, 154–173; Frank T. Denton, "The Significance of Significance: Rhetorical Aspects of Statistical Hypothesis Testing in Economics," in *The Consequences of Economic Rhetoric*, 163–183.

46. See Philip E. Converse, "The Nature of Belief Systems in Mass Publics," in *Ideology and Discontent*, ed. David Apter (New York: Free Press, 1964), 206–262.

47. See John S. Nelson, "The Ideological Connection, Parts I-II," *Theory and Society* 4, 3–4 (Fall–Winter 1977), 421–448 and 573–590.

CHAPTER TWO

Poetic History: Historical Experience, Nietzschean Genealogy, and Susan Daitch's *L.C.*

David W. Price

"Experience," writes Joan Scott, "is at once always already an interpretation *and* something that needs to be interpreted. What counts as experience is neither self-evident nor straight-forward; it is always contested, and always therefore political."[1] This closing remark, taken from Scott's powerful critique of the turn toward experience as a foundation for historical analysis, reminds us once again that historical "truth" emerges from a process of interpretive engagement with signifying systems, none of which can be used as an interpretive ground.

In recent years, the contestation of which Scott speaks has served as a primary field of intellectual inquiry that crosses over many disciplinary boundaries. The writings of historians such as Hayden White, Michel de Certeau, and Dominick LaCapra; literary critics such as Lionel Gossman and Linda Hutcheon; and novelists such as Robert Coover, E.L. Doctorow, Umberto Eco, Salman Rushdie, and Christa Wolf present rich and diverse approaches to questioning the nature of historical experience and its relationship to historical truth. For many of these writers, historical experience can only exist as it emerges from largely unacknowledged protocols of various discursive practices—be they philosophical, literary, economic, or mythological—which themselves govern both apprehension and expression.

The principal philosophical *éminence grise* who casts a shadow across the work of the above named writers, Scott included, is, of course, Friedrich Nietzsche. Indeed, his rejection of the very existence of "facts" and his declaration that "only interpretations" of phenomena exist[2] has become something of an article of faith among many contemporary theorists and historians. But to claim that there are only interpretations is not simply to say that all histories are lies. On the contrary, Nietzsche's position was perhaps best expressed in the title of his second untimely meditation: "On the Uses and Disadvantages of History for Life." Nietzsche's concern was to "learn better how to employ history for the purpose of life."[3] In other words, he sought to determine under what circumstances one should employ a certain type of history in order to make a truth that would enhance the "health of an individual, of a people and of a culture."[4]

As a form of intellectual inquiry, history is called upon to articulate the truth of the past. In the modern era, most historians believed that the key to uncovering historical truth lies in distinguishing "stories" from the past that are true from those that are false. This dichotomy of true and false, the common way of distinguishing the real and the fictive that undergirds the typical understanding of human experience, served as the focal point of Nietzsche's philosophical investigations. Rather than accept the standard dichotomy of true/false, Nietzsche, in an activity he termed genealogy, turned his attention to the constitutive properties and the concomitant *outcomes* of this and other dichotomies. In Nietzsche's estimation, to declare a judgment false does not automatically imply a rejection of that judgment. "The question," writes Nietzsche in *Beyond Good and Evil*, "is to what extent [the judgment] is life-promoting, life-preserving, species preserving, perhaps even species cultivating."[5]

Thus, in responding to the problem of history, truth, and expression in language, Nietzsche offered genealogy as a means to *make* the truths of history in order to meet certain political, social, or cultural needs in the present and for the future. The value of genealogy, therefore, lies in its utility in the *present*. Nietzschean genealogy, as Alan D. Schrift points out, emerges from the tension produced between Nietzsche's philosophy of perspectivism, which allows for various points of view, and his own adherence to principles of philological practice, which seeks verifiable truth. "[P]erspectival interpretation seem[s] to allow for an unbounded play of creative textual appropriation," writes Schrift, but "philological interpretation seems to call for methodological rigour and meticulous attention to the text itself."[6] It is this opposition that makes genealogy possible, such that it "appears to occupy a space between the interpretive demands of both philological attention and perspectival creativity."[7]

As we have already noted, the enhancement of life is the most important criterion governing genealogical practice. In this regard there are no "correct" interpretations; rather, there are those that either enhance or diminish life. The task of the historian, therefore, is to produce an interpretation, something we can characterize as a *poetic* act, which organizes different perspectives while at the same time employing philological rigor in pursuit of making a truth that will promote the life of the present culture.

Nietzsche's emphasis on the enhancement of life, however, is not limited to his history essay. Rather, the focus on "life" constitutes the central concern of his writings; but life, for Nietzsche, is inextricably bound to the concept of art, indeed, is the highest manifestation of the creative drive—we cannot separate art and life. From his early declaration in *The Birth of Tragedy* that "[i]t is only as an aesthetic phenomenon that existence and the world are eternally justified"[8] to his late characterization of the "world as a work of art that gives birth to itself,"[9] Nietzsche's writings offer us a sustained examination of the relationship between living and creating, between being an artist and being alive. In his monumental study of Nietzsche, Heidegger points out that it is precisely because art possesses a transfigurative capacity in contradistinction to the fixed quality of truth that Nietzsche sees in art its fundamental life-enhancing capability.[10] For Nietzsche, truth constitutes a "fixation of semblance"; art, however, "opens life up for creation of more life."[11] As Alexander Nehamas explains it, "Nietzsche's model for the world, for objects, and for people turns out to be the literary text and its components; his model for our relation to the world turns out to be interpretation."[12]

Nietzsche's insistence on the centrality of art and its relationship to truth is one of his most profound philosophical legacies. As an intellectual heir of Nietzsche, Scott pursues the line of analysis that focuses on that complex relation between truth and art. In her essay on "Experience," Scott calls for a type of reading that "would grant to 'the literary' an integral, even irreducible, status of its own." But she adds the following proviso: "To grant such status is not to make 'the literary' foundational, but to open new possibilities for analyzing discursive productions of social and political reality as complex, contradictory processes."[13] In other words, literature is not the ultimate source of knowledge that can provide us with all the answers to our questions, but it is a form of writing that offers us an excellent means of studying the activities of, and the various forms of writing produced by, the institutions of a given culture.

For Scott, the "literary" serves as a locus for examining discourse, one that affords us the opportunity to establish the interactive lines of filiation, cross-fertilization, and communication between the various forms of writing produced by the institutions of law, religion, science, business, medicine, politics, advertising, education, and economics, to name just a few. Literature as produced by writers such as Austen, Balzac, Dickens, Dostoyevsky, George Eliot, Stendhal, and Zola, for example, provides us with the means to discern how groups and individuals depicted in novels as well as the novelists themselves are influenced and in some cases dominated by the language and ideas of particular institutions. We can pause and consider how a character such as Dostoyevsky's Raskolnikov is caught in the grip of a contemporary philosophical or political idea or analyze the scientific metaphors used by Zola to describe the behaviors of mine workers in *Germinal.* In both cases we would gain insight into the periods depicted and the periods in which the works were written because we would be able to analyze, in the self-contained world of the literary text, the consequences of espousing these ideas or adopting these metaphors to describe the world. As readers we would also have the opportunity to see how these particular forms of writing were linked to other forms of discourse presented in the novel and to note how they reinforced or contradicted one another. In addition, in order to create their works, writers of literature must reduce complex material, pick and choose what to depict, symbolize ideas in the form of gesture and description, as well as reproduce speech patterns and organize their stories by adopting a particular plot. Scott reminds us that by studying literature we can begin to understand how we, too, must enact the processes of negation, condensation, appropriation, contradiction, and displacement that come into being when we *figure out* history in the form of a narrative.

When Scott emphasizes that this process of literary figuration, like the process of experience, is necessarily political, she thereby implies that the literary has value in that it is aware of its own figurative status, whereas neither experience nor other forms of discourse self-consciously acknowledge that they themselves emerge from antecedent chains of figuration. Scott challenges us to consider what we do when we recall an event that occurred in our own lives, something we call "experience." If, for example, you attempt to explain to a friend what happened to you in a car accident you will necessarily construct a story, and whether you acknowledge it or not, your "true" story will have many of the same structural devices that a fictional story would have. If the accident involves other cars, you may find yourself confronted with policemen and insurance investigators who will offer you diagrams and possible scenarios to help them put together a coherent story that will satisfactorily explain what took place. You may even find yourself in a court of law where advocates will debate who has put together the most plausible story. No one can deny that the cars collided and were damaged, but in the end you will be left with various versions or interpretations of what has happened. Each of these versions of the story, however, depends upon basic narrative plot devices, specialized languages associated with automotive engineering, law, and insurance claims adjustments, and imaginary constructs such as accident diagrams and coefficients of friction. Each narrator of the story must fit his or her tale into the diagrams provided by the insurance company or the skid mark analysis equations produced by police investigators. And each teller of the tale engages in politics because each teller has something to protect and promote (the insurance company may want to minimize costs, the police may want to stress the need for a light at the intersection where the accident took place, you may want to protect your reputation and not discuss how you were tired and had a few drinks earlier in the evening). In the end, there will be a "true" story: insurance companies will pay and reports will be filed, but *you* will have to choose which story to tell to your friend, the one that expresses the truth as you see it.

This lengthy example touches on the key, if complicated, point Scott makes. Even our everyday experience is governed by constructs. To appeal to experience means we must necessarily rely on narrative structural devices and imaginary constructs that are ordinarily found in fiction, and these devices and constructs have political ramifications. A significant argument that Scott emphasizes in her essay is that we don't acknowledge that we do depend on fictional devices to understand the truth of our experience. In a similar fashion, we fail to make the same acknowledgment when we discuss the narratives of history. Instead, we neatly divide the world between fact and fiction; we believe that the "story" or narrative of history presents an objective and apolitical truth. Scott, however, indicates that as a narrative form of truth-telling, history lacks self-awareness, and herein lies the value of literature: it recognizes its own fictional status. As Nietzsche would say, "[A]rt treats *illusion as illusion*; therefore it does not wish to deceive, it *is true.*"[14]

Although Scott's argument echoes much of Nietzsche's philosophy, she stops short of collapsing the distinction between fact and fiction. She would not claim, for example, that there is no difference between events that took place in World War II and those depicted in Norman Mailer's *The Naked and the Dead*. Nevertheless, when she declares that "[e]xperience is a subject's history," and "[l]anguage is the site of history's enactment," she is able to conclude that the literary may be an indispensable site of historical interpretation because historical explanation cannot afford to assume that it is possible to separate experience from language. Her purpose is not to promote what she calls "linguistic determinism"; rather, she wants "to insist . . . on the productive quality of discourse."[15] In other words, she seeks to engage in a critical examination of how competing discursive practices impinge upon, limit, support, further, thwart, explain, shape, (and themselves constitute) human experience; literature, she suggests, provides us with the best means to conduct such an examination.

Taken together then, Scott's call for a type of reading that grants the literary a special status finds its philosophical roots in Nietzschean genealogical practice; and the tension between philology and perspectivism that Schrift identifies as being the force field of genealogical production offers us a way of understanding Scott's proposed reading practice. Both Nietzsche and Scott suggest that the literary, by its very nature, enacts an interpretive activity that affords us the best opportunity to analyze the contentious discursive production of reality, that play of forces that genealogy exposes as being constitutive properties of the real. In the pages that follow, I will examine a number of contemporary works that illustrate the kind of conflicting interpretations and the genealogical method initiated by Nietzsche and promoted more recently by Scott.

At this point one might object and say that contemporary historians have acknowledged many of these same issues. Hayden White, of course, made his fellow historians acutely aware of the tropological underpinnings of every historical narrative. But White has never produced a historical narrative as such, his contributions have been strictly theoretical. Natalie Zemon Davis, by way of contrast, does produce historical narratives, and in the case of *The Return of Martin Guerre* she focuses specifically on individual experience. Nevertheless, her seamless narrative, which she admits "is in part my invention,"[16] does not display a contestation of interpretations. Despite two closing chapters of the book—"Histoire prodigieuse, Histoire tragique," which discusses the two earliest and most substantial versions of the Martin Guerre tale written by Jean de Coras and Guillaume Le Sueur, and "Of the Lame," which describes Michel de Montaigne's critique of Coras's judgment—Davis does not focus her primary attention on the different ways in which the tale has been interpreted. Instead, in the bulk of her book she produces her own eloquent, eminently readable prose, which provides us with a single (but not totalized) interpretation of the incident in Artigat. Even though the tale "retains a stubborn vitality," Davis characterizes herself as a "historian who has deciphered it."[17]

Perhaps *I, Pierre Rivière*, edited by Michel Foucault, provides us with the best example of a contemporary form of historiography that attempts to accomplish what I will claim Susan Daitch's novel succeeds in doing. Both Daitch and Foucault demonstrate how interpretation constitutes an act of poetic creation. Foucault's book, which examines the account of a nineteenth-century peasant who murdered his mother, sister, and brother, includes witness statements, medical and judicial reports, a narrative written by the accused himself, as well as analytical papers produced by eight members of a seminar conducted by Foucault at the Collège de France. The focus here is necessarily on discourse and its relation to truth. As Foucault explains in the forward,

> I think the reason we decided to publish these documents was to draw a map, so to speak, of those combats, to reconstruct these confrontations and battles, to rediscover the interaction of those discourses as weapons of attack and defense in the relations of power and knowledge.[18]

By reading this text, we learn that one medical examiner, a Dr. Bouchard, felt that the accused showed "no sign of mental derangement,"[19] whereas Dr. Vastel was "deeply and fully convinced that Rivière was not sane."[20] Armed with these and other contradictory observations made by the principal participants in the trial, Foucault's fellow seminar members draw some interesting conclusions of their own. Jean-Pierre Peter and Jeanne Faveret interpret Rivière's act as one of rebellion against the social order such that he felt he was "slaughtering a tyrant."[21] The institutions of social order, the authors argue, declared Rivière insane precisely because they wanted "to reduce the significance of his act; since it was aimed at the social order, the order of the contract, it could only be something done by a beast or a madman, the opposite of a man."[22] By granting Rivière a reprieve because he was insane, the authorities depoliticized his act. Interpreting the Rivière case in light of fly sheets, Foucault contends that these popular narratives of the time, describing acts of crime and punishment, commemorated "history below the level of power, one which clashed with the law."[23] Rather than focus on popular forms of discourse, Blandine Barret-Kriegel places the Rivière case in the realm of legal discourse. She examines the Rivière trial in the context of the regicide trial of Fieschi and argues that the Rivière verdict was affected by the Fieschi trial itself. Philippe Riot, however, examines the competing legal and medical discourses that make up part of the actual legal proceedings and concludes that the account of Rivière's life was used by doctors to demonstrate the accused's state of "mental deficiency" and this same account was used by the judges and prosecution to show that Rivière had never been mad.[24] For his part Riot observes a particular "break" in the Rivière narrative that makes it possible for the doctors and lawyers to produce their conflicting accounts.[25] Ultimately, Riot contends that the competing legal and medical accounts required that one disregard the memoir written by the accused himself.

In its entirety, the case of Pierre Rivière, as presented by Foucault, does touch on many of the elements I discussed earlier: perspectivism, interpretation as an act of creation, and language as the medium of historical truth production. It does not, however, focus specifically on the concept of experience, nor does it provide any detailed discussion of the relation between literature and history. Rather, *I, Pierre Rivière* offers an examination of some of the problems raised by Nietzsche, Scott, and Schrift at the level of institutional discursive practice.

When it comes to Scott's notion of the political dimension of historical narratives based on "experience," there are plenty of examples from which to choose. The recent academic controversy surrounding two interpretations of Captain James Cook's death in Hawaii offers us a telling example of the political dimension of any interpretation of a historical event. Two distinguished cultural anthropologists, Gananath Obeyesekere and Marshall Sahlins have produced accounts of Cook's encounter with the Hawaiians that reach very different conclusions about how the Hawaiians interpreted their experience. In 1982 and 1983 Sahlins delivered a series of lectures at Princeton University that focused on Polynesian War and Cook's death in Hawaii. With respect to the sea captain, Sahlins argued that Cook arrived on the island in 1778–79 during the Makahiki celebration period which commemorates the fertility god Lono. According to Sahlins, Cook arrived in the right place and at the right time to be taken as a manifestation of Lono himself. He even departed at the proper time, but when he was forced to return to the island to make repairs to his vessel, the Hawaiians saw this as a crisis in the very structure of the order of their world and their logical response was to kill Cook and put their world aright.

Obeyesekere rejects this view in *The Apotheosis of Captain Cook: European Mythmaking in the Pacific*, claiming that Sahlins's interpretation is a form of mythmaking on the part of Europeans. For Obeyesekere, the idea that the "Natives" looked upon Cook as a god is a myth invented by eighteenth-century Europeans themselves. "To put it bluntly," he writes, "I doubt that the natives created their European god; the Europeans created him for them. This 'European god' is a myth of conquest, imperialism, and civilization—a triad that cannot be easily separated."[26] Obeyesekere views the Hawaiians as being much more pragmatic; Sahlins, he contends, prefers to look upon them as irrational primitives, an interpretation that helps to support the cultural imperialism of the West. The evidence Sahlins adduces in support of his interpretation, claims Obeyesekere, includes the following arguments: 1) the Hawaiians viewed Cook's ship as a manifestation of Lono's canoe; 2) when the English sailor Watman died and was buried, the Hawaiians perceived him as the victim that was required to be sacrificed as part of the Makahiki festival; and 3) when the English sailors dismantled the Makahiki shrine and used it for firewood, the Hawaiians interpreted this as part of the ritual dismantling of the shrine that occurred every year. Obeyesekere's response to this is as lucid as it is terse:

> I think it quite improbable that the Hawaiians could not make a distinction between the physical shape of Lono's tiny canoe that

> is floated at the conclusion of Makahiki and Cook's great ships, or that for them the corpse of Watman was a sacrificial victim, or that marines dismantling the palings of the shrine for firewood was a ritual dismantling of the sort practiced by their own priests. One has to balance the facts of physical perception with cultural reality and what I have called "practical rationality."[27]

In *How "Natives" Think: About Captain Cook, for Example* (which consists of 285 pages of text including seventeen appendices), Sahlins presents a devastating and sometimes acrimonious rebuttal to Obeyesekere's critique. Accusing Obeyesekere of adopting an "inverted enthocentrism" that ends in "an anti-anthropology,"[28] Sahlins contends that the "central critical vision of Obeyesekere's book" yields the following: "the Hawaiians are endowed with the highest form of Western mentality, while Western scholars slavishly repeat the irrational beliefs of their ancestors."[29] Sahlins takes Obeyesekere to task for "[p]resuming that as a native Sri Lankan he has a privileged insight into how Hawaiians thought."[30] As a result, in Sahlins's view, Obeyesekere's "underlying thesis is crudely unhistorical, a not-too-implicit notion that all natives so-called (by Europeans) are alike, most notably in their common cause for resentment."[31]

In a chapter entitled "Historical Fiction, Makeshift Ethnography," Sahlins argues that Obeyesekere "fail[ed] to consider the Hawaiians' theological doctrines";[32] instead, he produced an analysis in which "Hawaiian theology is understood on the basis of (alleged) Sri Lankan notions of gods and their worldly forms."[33] In short, Sahlins asserts that by "[s]electively ignoring or misrepresenting the primary documents, he [Obeyesekere] constructs an implausible history out of a habitual combination of commonsense realism and pop anthropology."[34]

Both of these respected anthropologists amass evidence in support of their arguments, and both offer eloquent defenses of their respective positions. The political implications of each of their positions are quite obvious, and we as readers are left to choose. The truth about Cook in Hawaii, it seems, is a matter of interpretation. The debate between Sahlins and Obeyesekere, however, underscores Scott's major point, namely, that interpretation based on experience (in this case the experience of other peoples as interpreted by anthropologists) is never transparent and is always inflected with a deeply political dimension.

Rather than rely on historians for a thorough understanding of the complexities associated with contestatory interpretations, the limits of experiential knowledge, and the grounds of truth, it is incumbent upon us to turn to literature, to see in what ways history *is* literature, for it is literature that allows us to examine these issues in a space that Wendy Steiner describes as a "virtual realm tied to the world by acts of interpretation."[35] As Paul de Man said, literature "is the only form of language free from the fallacy of unmediated expression"[36] and as such it provides us with the perfect ground for investigating the very concept of interpretive mediation via linguistic expression. In this regard, Susan Daitch's novel *L.C.* is the ideal narrative to conduct our investigation of these matters.

I have selected *L.C.* (1986) for five reasons. First, *L.C.* concerns itself with the writing of history as based upon individual experience. Second, the novel focuses specifically on women's experience in history and feminist historical practice, something that is central to Scott's own analysis. Third, the novel has (surprisingly) received scant critical attention. Linda Hutcheon has offered a handful of illuminating pages on Daitch's novel in two books on postmodernism and what she terms "historiographic metafiction," and a special 1993 edition of the *Review of Contemporary Fiction* devoted four articles to Daitch's work. Fourth, *L.C.* is very much a novel about writing and translation, as well as history, and all three are key concepts in Nietzsche's writings. Finally, and most important of all, *L.C.* presents us with a clear understanding of Nietzsche's claim that the truths of history are linguistic constructs, that they are products of poetic acts which we use in order to meet specific needs in the present. The following analysis will demonstrate how Daitch's novel presents an interpretation of competing readings of a history based upon "experience." Using both Scott's and Schrift's work as my interpretive analytic framework, I will show how Daitch's approach consists of enacting a Nietzschean genealogical method that puts into play philological interpretation and, in Schrift's words, perspectival "creative textual appropriation."[37] In this regard I argue that Daitch makes manifest Schrift's particular interpretation of the genealogical method, one characterized by a tension between perspectival free play and philological rigor. I will also argue that *L.C.* unequivocally demonstrates Scott's major point about the fallacy of appealing to experience as a ground for historical interpretation. By employing the work of Scott and Schrift as two interpretive lenses, one can see how Daitch, through a work of fiction, offers us insight into Nietzsche's understanding of history as a series of constructed truths, *in language*, designed to meet specific and often competing cultural and political needs.

At first glance, *L.C.* appears to be a type of historical novel that presents itself as a genuine historical artifact containing both the journal entries of Lucienne Crozier, a participant in the revolution of 1848 in Paris, as well as an introduction and explanatory notes provided by the translator of the journal, Dr. Willa Rehnfield. Lucienne's diary, as translated by Rehnfield, records the impressions of a young woman who had an affair with the painter Eugène Delacroix, joined the revolutionary group *14 Juillet* and, after the failure of the 1848 revolution, eventually escaped to North Africa with one of the group's leaders, Jean de la Tour, only to succumb to tuberculosis and die.

About one hundred pages into the novel, a second editor, a certain Jane Amme, who we later learn was an assistant to Rehnfield, provides six additional explanatory notes, two of which critique the Rehnfield translation and two more of which seek to clarify what Rehnfield has written. The reader next discovers that Jane Amme has a particular story to tell that is independent from, yet intimately related to, the Crozier story and that *L.C.* itself is much more than a novel disguised as historical document. The second editor, Jane, offers an "Epilogue" in the middle of *L.C.* that explains how Rehnfield obtained the journal, and how she, Jane, became an editorial assistant to Rehnfield and eventually the executor of Rehnfield's will.

Jane Amme, it turns out, is the *nom de guerre* of a former '60s revolutionary who survived the battles of Berkeley (1968–72), and was forced to go underground after she killed a man who had raped her. The rapist, Luc Ferrier, was also an industrialist who had reaped huge profits from the sale of war materials used during the Vietnam conflict. When Jane kills Ferrier with a firebomb, the press concludes that antiwar activists murdered him. In order to avoid arrest, Jane travels east and begins to work for Rehnfield and later learns that this same Ferrier was the person who helped Rehnfield obtain the Crozier diary when he bought some Delacroix paintings on the black market and had them smuggled into the United States.

Daitch's novel then takes yet another surprising turn when Jane offers her own translation of the last few months' entries in the Crozier diary. Jane's translation differs markedly from Rehnfield's and conveys Amme's repudiation of Rehnfield's historical methodology, her political ideology, and her understanding of the French language.

Taken in its entirety, therefore, Daitch's novel records the experiences of three women: a woman during the revolution of 1848, a woman student radical of the 1960s, and a traditionally trained historian. By presenting her readers with two translations of a historical document—one by the traditional historian Rehnfield and the other by a '60s radical—Daitch's novel records an interpretive contest between a historian who is dependent upon what we might term a *grand récit*, or grand narrative, and a person practicing Nietzschean genealogy.

Dr. Rehnfield represents a member of a growing body of historians who look to the particulars of everyday life in order to learn "what really happened" in the past. She resembles those historians who, according to Scott, issue a "challenge to normative history" by resting their "claim to legitimacy on the authority of experience" in order to correct "oversights resulting from innacurate or incomplete vision."[38] Precisely because a diary contains the language of personal experience, a language she uncritically accepts as being wholly transparent, Rehnfield believes that such a document can make a positive contribution to our understanding of the past. In other words, Lucienne's "experience" becomes foundational for Rehnfield; but it in *no way challenges the larger view of the past.* For Dr. Rehnfield, historical truth is *found*, and it is corroborated by supporting evidence gathered from the past, but this evidence constitutes elements of a larger historical pattern that is already understood. The diary, as Rehnfield interprets it, simply augments and affirms a received understanding of the nineteenth century. Her entire interpretation is circumscribed by certain meaning-producing, grand narratives of the nineteenth century that are received wisdom from the fields of sociology, political science, epidemiology, and demography. Thus, Lucienne's times, according to Rehnfield, were shaped by figures such as Daumier, Balzac, Napoleon, Talleyrand, King Louis-Philippe, and Guizot. In Rehnfield's hands, therefore, Lucienne becomes a metonymic exemplar of what we already "know" about nineteenth-century experience as produced by social, economic, and political discourses.

For Jane, however, historical truth is not found; it is made. Like Nietzsche, Jane recognizes that historical truths are made through the interpretive act, and these interpretations can and ought to be useful in the present. Jane's truth emerges from her act of translating the diary, as she begins to understand Lucienne's experience in 1848 through her own experience in the revolutionary movement of the 1960s. In many ways, Jane sees her own life as a repetition of Crozier's experience within a revolutionary movement. Both the male revolutionaries of

1968 and the male *Quarante-huitards* fought for social equality but refused to extend equal rights to women within their own revolutionary groups. The parallels between the two revolutionary movements cannot be denied. Indeed, the central feminist thrust of the novel hinges on the reader's recognition that if the old French adage "plus ça change, plus c'est la même chose" still holds true, it remains true with respect to the position of women in society in general, and in revolutionary movements in particular, *because* the position of women has been stabilized through social fictions (what Foucault would term discursive practices) taken to be true or natural. Jane's translation of the Crozier diary and the narration of her own experiences, which echo Lucienne's, serve as a genealogical critique aimed at uncovering (or destabilizing) the social fictions that have governed the representation of women's experiences in history.

By offering her own footnotes and by translating a portion of the Crozier diary herself, Jane constructs a perspective in opposition to Rehnfield's. First, she employs philological rigor and points out how Rehnfield would often make errors in translation by resorting to anachronistic expressions. For example, Jane indicates that Rehnfield uses the concept of the picket line before it came into existence.[39] Similarly, Rehnfield claims that the *14 Juillet* group was making dynamite a full eighteen years before Alfred Nobel had invented it.[40] According to Jane, "Dr. Rehnfield pressed her passages over the lines" of Lucienne's diary and turned it into "a blurry palimpsest." For Jane, Rehnfield's "language has become L. Crozier's, her framing intrudes into the picture, her involvement with the papers has become part of what the diary is."[41]

> As she continued to study the Rehnfield translation of the Crozier diary, Jane began to consider what the translator skipped, blanched at and erased, or forgot to include altogether, as if by accident. It's a lacuna the eye ignored because the overall pattern was taken for granted—suddenly the gap stood out and became the whole text, the whole story.[42]

In other words, Rehnfield approached the diary with a preconceived "overall pattern," a *grand récit* of sorts, that *determined the perspective* that emerges from the translation. Rehnfield sought merely to "enlarge the picture," as Scott would say, but her horizon of interpretive possibilities is limited by the received ideas of narratives of nineteenth-century history. By appealing to the experience of Crozier as a confirmation of the historical narrative, Rehnfield's approach suffers from a fundamental flaw because, as Scott points out, "the project of making experience visible precludes critical examination of the workings of the ideological system itself, its categories of representation . . . its premises about what these categories mean and how they operate."[43]

Jane's approach toward the diary differs from Rehnfield's dramatically. Language, what Scott calls "the site of history's enactment,"[44] serves as Jane's primary field of investigation as she produces her own translation of the Crozier diary. "Translation," as Jane correctly observes, "is a filter, there is always some refraction."[45] With this in mind, Jane rejects Rehnfield's interpretation and selects her own filter by attending to the particularities of language in order to articulate her own perspective, a perspective that seeks to enhance life as Nietzsche suggested.

In her most stunning deviation from the Rehnfield translation, and one that directly challenges Rehnfield's method, Jane reads Lucienne's diary figuratively rather than literally. In an entry dated 5 August 1848, Lucienne describes what she calls her "quarantine" in North Africa.[46] Complaining bitterly that Jean de la Tour's "ideas exist and thrive exclusive of female contribution," Lucienne decides that rather than accept Jean's invitation to meet S., she would prefer to "remain in quarantine." Unlike Rehnfield who accepts language as being contextualized in an already articulated narrative of the past (i.e., any use of the term quarantine refers to the larger pattern of the nineteenth-century outbreak of tuberculosis), Jane chooses to read the passage figuratively. Jane's Lucienne does not suffer from tuberculosis; rather, she is a victim of the repressive society of North Africa that forbids women to go freely out of doors.

Only by dressing as men can she and her friend Pascale see the society that has welcomed Jean de la Tour and the other exiled revolutionaries. In the context of the passages translated by Jane, phrases such as "remain in quarantine" and "I'm treated like a chronic invalid"[47] serve as metaphors to describe what Lucienne felt like when she was denied permission to move freely in North African society. For Jane, Lucienne employs an illness metaphor to describe both her personal condition and the chronic ailment of her culture—namely, inequality between the sexes. Jane's figurative reading receives confirmation at the end of the diary when Lucienne shows her conscious use of sickness metaphors by concluding the 13 November entry with the following lines: "Sickness is ensured, I have been exposed to contagion, in this case fear of arrest and prison."[48] The repressive society, not biological disease, triggers Lucienne's play of language. Jane's method of reading the diary figuratively confirms Nietzsche's dicta that all language is "a movable host of metaphors,"[49] and that "[t]he world with which we are concerned is false, i.e., is not a fact but a fable and approximation on the basis of a meager sum of observations."[50]

But Jane's emphasis on the figurative should not surprise us once we pause and reconsider what Lucienne consistently says throughout the diary—even in the portions of it translated by Rehnfield. The diary opens with Lucienne recalling an eccentric woman named Mlle Pitou who told a fable about three shepherdesses in perpetual mourning: one longed for the past, one for the present, and one for the future. Lucienne then details a conversation she had many years later, on board a train, with an old woman who reminds her of Mlle Pitou. The old woman relates the story of the railroad bridge that is haunted by the spirits of two women and a man who were mysteriously murdered there during the Reign of Terror. Each of the three souls longed for a particular time; one mourned for the past, one for the present, and one for the future. Upon hearing the story, Lucienne concludes that she would mourn for the present.

When Lucienne observes that the "Mademoiselle Pitous of the world . . . carry on the private history of each department of France,"[51] we as readers should recognize the traditionally established dichotomy of private and public history, wherein the former is either marginalized (e.g., everyone remembers the Reign of Terror but no one knows the truth about these three people) or made to serve as a distorting lens such that in Lucienne's words, "Over the generations the history turns into tales."[52] In this regard, Daitch's novel reminds us that historical narratives, even those focused on common individuals, often obscure the particularities and idiosyncrasies of an individual's life in order to show how this individual exemplifies the larger patterns of belief and social practice which we believe were dominant at that time. In short, historical narratives can make the individual disappear into a larger construct of "history" such that we do not really get to see and understand the complex and contradictory nature of a human being who lived in the past. Thus, the "Pitou" vignettes announce a central theme of the novel: the private history of Lucienne will be related to the larger story of the events of 1848, and depending upon what perspective (what "translation") one adopts, Lucienne's private history will either confirm the larger narrative of history or critique and contradict it.

By declaring her preference for mourning for the present, Lucienne expresses not only her concern for living in the here and now, but also her interest in what Nietzsche terms the formation of values. Nowhere is this more clearly expressed than in the diary passages that reflect on or describe certain art and artists. As her diary repeatedly indicates, Lucienne views the interpretive schemes adopted by artists with grave suspicion because what informs those interpretations is never fully articulated.

"I'm not impressed by mirrors of nature," Luicienne writes.[53] The typical painting of "still life" does not reveal a truth; rather, it presents what is always already known. Such re-presentations of the given reproduce already accepted descriptions of the "real" and confirm an ontology predicated upon an unacknowledged epistemology. The focus of such art is on a state of being rather than a moment of becoming. It is little wonder, then, that the French refer to "still life" as *la nature morte*. As viewers of such art, we already know what we are looking at; our preconceptions are confirmed, the interpetation foreclosed. These so-called "mirrors of nature" depict the world as having reached a final state. But as Nietzsche argues, the world "does not aim at a final state";[54] rather, the world is in a state of becoming.

Lucienne's preference for becoming as opposed to being attracts her to the work of Eugène Delacroix. When she first sees his painting of a Turk about to spear a leopard, she is struck by the lack of resolution in the scene. The action is suspended; the Turk may kill the leopard or the "cunning" animal may in fact kill the Turk. In her first attempts to interpret the canvas, Lucienne calls upon her familiarity with depictions of St. George and the dragon. Her initial reflex is to superimpose an already articulated Western narrative similar to, but not identical with, the one she encounters. This method of interpretation, however, does not work. "St. George is the historic victor," she writes, "but with regard to the little Turk it's not clear."[55] In what ultimately can be construed as an Orientalist perspective, Lucienne nevertheless sees in Delacroix's canvas a supratemporal moment that paradoxically captures a state of becoming; no prior narrative can offer the viewer an interpretive grid because the scene Delacroix presents is in flux, whereas the interpretive paradigm of St. George is self-contained, closed off, or in Lucienne's words, "historic."

Lucienne's preference for Delacroix's approach receives confirmation when she views the work of Rémy Gommereux, a practicing "new realist." Gommereux claims his realism is "all inclusive." But as Lucienne points out, "His realism isn't simply an all-inclusive mirror. There are schemes of elimination, the encyclopaedic impulse is often only a glib repetition of ideas that are in the Parisian air."[56] Put simply, Gommereux leaves things out; he embellishes his paintings with received ideas. His documentary impulse and his obsession with drawing never fill the lacunae inherent in his representations of the real world. It is no accident that his name, Gommereux, contains the word for eraser (*gomme*).

Lucienne's recognition that a "realist" technique based upon former narratives does not offer valid representations of the "real world" parallels Jane's rejection of Rehnfield's interpretive approach, one that could be characterized as both "realistic" and dependent upon former narrative truths. In both cases, Gommereux and Rehnfield, despite what they may think, actually *make* their respective truths, and thus they can be said to engage in poetic acts. Nietzsche himself characterized all attempts at capturing the "real" as the work of "we spiders" who sit in our net. "[W]hatever we may catch in it," writes Nietzsche, "we catch nothing at all except that which allows itself to be caught in precisely *our* net."[57] From Jane's perspective, Rehnfield spins a web of meanings that catches what she is looking for, namely, an individual who embodies the grand narratives of the nineteenth century. Rehnfield denies the poetic nature of her constructed history because she believes that she is reproducing an objective view of the past. Jane rejects such a view, and the key to her response to Rehnfield lies in her understanding of Lucienne's recognition of the truth of art, the supratemporal art of Delacroix.

Just as Lucienne looked upon the Delacroix painting and engaged in a creative interpretive act by rejecting the St. George paradigm offered by her culture, Jane rejects the interpretive grids offered by established history and chooses to read the Crozier diary creatively. Through her translation, Jane creates her own past through a poetic act of making that establishes the continuity between Lucienne's experience and her own. Her goal is to examine the ideologies that determined her "experience." Unlike Rehnfield, who simply admits that the *Quarante-huitards* were sexists and leaves it at that, Jane wants to uncover what assumptions led to the repeated failure of revolutionary movements. For Jane the answer is quite clear: so-called revolutionaries, to this day, adhere to ideologies that conceive of women as being subservient. The attitude of the men of 1848, an attitude that led to the immediate rejection of Pascale's ideas during clandestine meetings in Paris, repeats itself in 1968 when Win, a Berkeley radical, regards Jane as a submissive sex partner, a nurse maid, and a typist. In other words, both sets of revolutionaries failed to see gender as a power relation.

Through her juxtaposition of two perspectives on history within the boundaries of a novel and through her emphasis on the importance of philological attentiveness, Daitch creates an interpretation of history that simultaneously shows us how historical reality results from contradictory discursive production processes. Thus, the two temporal plains (1848 and 1968) under scrutiny in Daitch's novel are represented in two ways. They are traditionally represented through already understood historical narratives that reduce the semantic possibilities available to readers of historical texts. As we have seen, when Rehnfield limits her understanding of "quarantine" to the semantic field of illness, she thereby occludes the metaphoric potential of the word. Similarly, the journalistic explanation of the bombing of Luc Ferrier appeals to the grand antiwar narrative which obscures the story of Jane's rape. Yet, in her presentation of counternarratives, the second manner of historical representation, Daitch's novel underscores the necessity of a philological rigor in pursuit of making history useful, one that does not so much seek to unmask the "truth" or the essence of history as it does to contribute to life. "Rigorous philology," writes Sarah Kofman, "unmasks interpretation as interpretation in the name of an other interpretation which does not pretend to grasp the essence of being but which offers a revelatory reading of a life affirming will" (*my translation*).[58] Daitch's novel leaves us with nothing *but* interpretations; we do not read the original French journals of Lucienne. We do not even know if such manuscripts exist in our (the reader's) world. Nor would it matter.

For Daitch's novel suggests that when it comes to history there are only poetic interpretations. Like Nietzsche, she believes that we must choose interpretations that contribute to the health of our culture. Daitch also confirms Scott's claim that the literary is a key locus for understanding historical reality. *L.C.* performs the very analysis of the "discursive productions of social and political reality" that Scott calls for, and shows them to be "complex, contradictory processes."[59] *L.C.* calls for a reevaluation of revolutionary politics and points to a reconceptualization of such politics in order to bring about substantive change. The title itself signals this call to the reader. The homonymous reading of the title *in French* would signify, in addition to the letters of the alphabet, a terse declarative sentence: *Elle sait* (She knows). But herein lies the irreducible ambiguity of the novel and, concomitantly, history, particularly history based upon experience. For in truth who is "she"? and in fact, what does she "know"? The answers to these questions can only emerge through the interpretive act, one that involves the interplay of philological rigor and perspectival free play even as it acknowledges that such acts are always contested and always political.

Daitch's novel enacts the problematic of producing a history. Like Nietzsche, Daitch recognizes that certain types of history are necessary if a culture is to survive. In this regard, Jane's translation offers the greatest hope for interpreting the past so as to affect the future and improve the position of women in society. Like Scott, Daitch acknowledges that no ground exists, least of all experience, upon which one can build a history. The somber, some would say ominous, ending of the novel underscores the realization that the interpretive process never reaches a final state, that it never escapes contestation, that it always remains within the field of politics.

With respect to feminist historical practice, *L.C.* articulates a more direct response. When Daitch the novelist has Rehnfield confine sexist behavior to the past, contextualize Crozier's language in the already given grand narrative of nineteenth-century France, and base her research on documents obtained from a rapist and industrialist who embodies the controlling political power structures of the present age, she presents a damning indictment of contemporary historians—even historians of so-called "Women's History"—who still cling to the notion that historiographic methodology based upon "evidence" obtained through "experience" reveals the "truth." Such an approach, Daitch suggests, is simply misguided and in many ways remains complicitous with the very power structures that perpetuate social inequalities which persist to this day. It is Jane's approach that allows her to *make* her own truth and, in doing so, further life.

Through her novel, Daitch reveals the constitutive discursivity of the real. Her fiction recapitulates the figuration of all forms of history and echoes Nietzsche's understanding that we "must organize the chaos within [us] by thinking back to [our] real needs."[60] Daitch, like Scott, refuses to separate "experience" and language. *L.C.* shows us the conflicts, contradictions, and multiple meanings produced by competing discourses, and in so doing, confirms Scott's notion that "the literary" can "open new possibilities" for analyzing history.

NOTES

1. Joan W. Scott, "The Evidence of Experience," *Critical Inquiry* 19 (1991): 797.

2. Friedrich Nietzsche, *The Will to Power*, trans. Walter Kaufmann and R.J. Hollingdale (New York: Vintage, 1968), para. 481.

3. Friedrich Nietzsche, "On the Uses and Disadvantages of History for Life," *Untimely Meditations*, trans. R.J. Hollingdale (Cambridge: Cambridge University Press, 1990), 66.

4. Nietzsche, "On the Uses and Disadvantages of History for Life," 63.

5. Friedrich Nietzsche, *Beyond Good and Evil*, trans. Walter Kaufmann (New York: Vintage, 1966), 11.

6. Alan D. Schrift, "Between Perspectivism and Philology: Genealogy as Hermeneutic," *Nietzsche-Studien* 16 (1987): 104.

7. Schrift, "Between Perspectivism and Philology: Genealogy as Hermeneutic," 108.

8. Friedrich Nietzsche, *The Birth of Tragedy*, trans. Walter Kaufmann (New York: Vintage, 1967), 52.

9. Nietzsche, *The Will To Power*, para. 796.

10. Martin Heidegger, *Nietzsche: The Will to Power as Art*, trans. David Farrell Krell (San Francisco: Harper Collins Paperback, 1991), 216–217.

11. Alan D. Schrift, *Nietzsche and The Question of Interpretation: Between Hermeneutics and Deconsrtuction* (New York: Routledge, 1990), 50.

12. Alexander Nehamas, *Nietzsche: Life as Literature* (Cambridge: Harvard University Press, 1985), pp. 90–91.

13. Scott, "The Evidence of Experience," 793–794.

14. Friedrich Nietzsche, "On Truth and Lies in the Nonmoral Sense," in *Philosophy and Truth: Selections from Nietzsche's Notebooks of the Early 1870's*, ed. Daniel Brezeale (Atlantic Highlands, N.J.: Humanities Press, 1990), 96.

15. Scott, "The Evidence of Experience," 793.

16. Natalie Zemon Davis, *The Return of Martin Guerre* (Cambridge: Harvard University Press, 1983), 5.

17. Davis, *The Return of Martin Guerre*, 125.

18. Michel Foucault, ed., *I, Pierre Rivière, having slaughtered my mother, my sister and my brother . . . : A Case of Parricide in the 19th Century*. trans. Frank Jellinek (New York: Pantheon Books, 1975), xi.

19. Michel Foucault, ed., *I, Pierre Rivière*, 124.

20. Michel Foucault, ed., *I, Pierre Rivière*, 125.

21. Michel Foucault, ed., *I, Pierre Rivière*, 191.

22. Michel Foucault, ed., *I, Pierre Rivière*, 193.

23. Michel Foucault, ed., *I, Pierre Rivière*, 205.

24. Michel Foucault, ed., *I, Pierre Rivière*, 232.

25. Michel Foucault, ed., *I, Pierre Rivière*, 235.

26. Gananath Obeyesekere, *The Apotheosis of Captain Cook: European Mythmaking in the Pacific* (Princeton: Princeton University Press, 1992), 3.

27. Obeyesekere, *The Apotheosis of Captain Cook: European Mythmaking in the Pacific*, 60.

28. Marshall Sahlins, *How "Natives" Think: About Captain Cook, For Example* (Chicago: Chicago University Press, 1995), 151.

29. Sahlins, *How "Natives" Think: About Captain Cook, For Example*, 9.

30. Sahlins, *How "Natives" Think: About Captain Cook, For Example*, 1.

31. Sahlins, *How "Natives" Think: About Captain Cook, For Example*, 5.

32. Sahlins, *How "Natives" Think: About Captain Cook, For Example*, 122.

33. Sahlins, *How "Natives" Think: About Captain Cook, For Example*, 120.

34. Sahlins, *How "Natives" Think: About Captain Cook, For Example*, 117.

35. Wendy Steiner, *The Scandal of Pleasure: Art in an Age of Fundamentalism* (Chicago: Chicago University Press, 1995), 8.

36. Paul De Man, *Blindness and Insight: Essays in the Rhetoric of Contemporary Criticism*. 2nd ed. (Minneapolis: University of Minnesota Press, 1983), 17.

37. Schrift, "Between Perspectivism and Philology: Genealogy as Hermeneutic," 105.

38. Scott, "The Evidence of Experience," 776.

39. Susan Daitch, *L.C.* (New York: Harcourt, 1986), 114.

40. Daitch, *L.C.*, 220.

41. Daitch, *L.C.*, 163.

42. Daitch, *L.C.*, 164.

43. Scott, "The Evidence of Experience," 778.

44. Scott, "The Evidence of Experience," 793.

45. Daitch, *L.C.*, 171–172.

46. Daitch, *L.C.*, 272.

47. Daitch, *L.C.*, p 269.

48. Daitch, *L.C.*, 281.

49. Nietzsche, "On Truth and Lies in the Nonmoral Sense," 84.

50. Nietzsche, *The Will to Power*, para. 616.

51. Daitch, *L.C.*, 15.

52. Daitch, *L.C.*, 15.

53. Daitch, *L.C.*, 24.

54. Nietzsche, *The Will to Power*, para. 708.

55. Daitch, *L.C.*, 24.

56. Daitch, *L.C.*, 86.

57. Friedrich Nietzsche, *Daybreak*, trans. R. J. Hollingdale (Cambridge: Cambridge University Press, 1982), 73.

58. Sarah Kofman, *Nietzsche et la métaphor* (Paris: Éditions Galilée, 1983), 204.

59. Scott, "The Evidence of Experience," 794.

60. Nietzsche, "On the Uses and Disadvantages of History for Life," 123.

CHAPTER THREE

"Gigantic Shadows of Futurity"

History and Politics in Shelley's *Defence of Poetry*

Jacqueline LeBlanc

As a poet and political activist, Percy Bysshe Shelley was at the center of Modernity's debate between the poetic and the rational. A disciple of William Godwin, Shelley regarded himself the heir to Enlightenment revolutionaries and 1790s radicals. As a poet, however, Shelley was also at odds with this tradition's struggle to free society and government from poetic myths in the name of rational truth. Shelley, instead, saw a continuum between political emancipation and poetic creativity. He rejected the rationalist precept that the world is a fixed phenomenon that needs to be discovered. Instead, Shelley understood history and politics as poetic constructions. He is thus a precursor to the Nietzschean conception of history as poiesis, the active *creation* of useful forms of existence.

Shelley repudiated the notion that poetry is merely a product of historical forces. Poetry, he believed, reflects a transformation brewing in the social/political environment and *spurs* this transformation. He wrote in his Preface to *Prometheus Unbound* (1820): "The great writers of our own age are . . . the companions and forerunners of some unimagined change in our social condition or the opinions which cement it. . . . Poets . . . are, in one sense, the creators, and in another, the creations of their age."[1] Shelley contends here that poetry and history influence each other mutually: while historical change causes new poetry, new poetry equally causes historical change.

As Shelley developed and expanded this philosophy one year later in *A Defence of Poetry* this reciprocal conception of poetry and history emerges as a far more radical proposition. In his *Defence* Shelley reiterates his opinion that poets are both the "followers" and the "heralds" of political reform, but he also radically extends it by defining history as poetry. This chapter will explain what I see as two broad rhetorical delineations in Shelley's philosophy that define history as poetic representation: first, Shelley's politicizing of aesthetic form, and second, his aestheticizing of politics and history. Shelley argues, in his *Defence*, that poetry is a reformist force in history, and that history itself is a poetic construction. The latter becomes a means to arguing the former, but aestheticizing history also contributes to a complex understanding of history as more than a fixed origin or empirical context. History is a human interpretation, a "creation" of the past, present, and future. History, Shelley argues, is a poem because poetry is a force of change. Yet his argument also implies that history is a written record of itself. We cannot untangle events of the past from the form in which we interpret them. History is a poem because it is not simply recorded; it is "invented."[2]

Young Shelley as Revolutionary

As a poet, then, Shelley saw himself equally as a politician, as a "creator" of his age. Indeed, in 1812, the year following his expulsion from Oxford, Shelley assumed the role not of poet, but of political activist, embarking on a revolutionary campaign to Dublin, where he hoped to aid the Catholic rebellion against British rule. Following his own ideal interpretation of the American and French Revolutions, Shelley saw himself as a Thomas Paine figure, eager to precipitate a "quiet revolution" through distributing *Common Sense*–like pamphlets.[3]

As Shelley understood it, his mission in Dublin was to reinvent politics. Like many intellectuals of his period, Shelley felt a conflict between politics as practiced (according to both the establishment and the reformists) and the politics of his moral vision. Shelley rebelled against his family's wishes that he pursue a career in Parliament since he could not morally abide by his government's unjust practices. Perhaps in disgust with the corruption he observed in British government, Shelley decided in 1811 "that political affairs are quite distinct from morality, that they cannot be united."[4] His definition of poetry as reformist political praxis in the *Defence of Poetry* ten years later would be his final means of moralizing politics by inventing a politically reformist vision outside of the traditional political system. Shelley's mission in Dublin, however, was his first attempt at overcoming his perceived gap between morality and politics, and he did so not by writing a poem, but by attempting to involve himself directly with the commoners and the political groups that represented Irish nationalism.

Shelley had discovered, between his pessimism of 1811 and his optimism of 1812, William Godwin's *Enquiry Concerning Political Justice* (1793) and found there a hope for a politics "which would allow moral values to become operative in the real world."[5] Godwin's political philosophy favored education over government as the true site of political reform, and thus he introduced the potential for a poetic politics, a politics of literature and letters outside of the government Shelley reviled. At the same time, Godwin provided an answer to—as Shelley perceived—the greatest political tragedies of his age, the Reign of Terror and Napoleonic rule. Writing a generation after Paine and Godwin, Shelley found that his own radical politics should identify with the ideals of the Revolution but must also resist its mistakes. By 1812, Shelley had come to the conclusion that France during the Revolution lacked sufficient men and women "of enlightened minds and unselfish spirits to guide the French into more constructive paths."[6] It was the violence of despotism, he believed, that evoked the counterdespotism of the Terror and Napoleon.[7] He sought to avoid this pattern in Ireland by, as he saw it, spreading enlightenment rather than inciting violent protest. In Ireland, Shelley saw himself as awakening the *imagination* of the masses, something he considered quite distinct from the rationalist scientific approach of Enlightenment political reform. For Shelley, imagination creates empathy even as it brings emancipation, while science produces freedom only through cold reason. Shelley believed strongly in an opposition between the nature of violent war and that of the imagination. While he recognized the aesthetic quality of "the pageantry of arms and badge," he contended that this propagandistic display "corrupts the imagination of men."[8] Shelley located true reform not in armed revolt but in transforming the imaginative consciousness of humankind. Thus, Shelley wrote to Godwin in discouragement of the unchanged political structure in England since Godwin set down his philosophy of reform in his *Enquiry* in 1793: "I think of the last twenty years with patient skepticism as to the progress which the human mind has made during this period."[9] Even during these early years of political activism we see the origins of Shelley's politics of poetry. His newfound moral politics is a politics of the imagination—of "the human mind"—the only politics, he believed, sufficiently divorced from establishment and radical violence to allow for human freedom. His first attempt at enacting his moral politics, however, failed. Shelley's proposals proved incompatible with the structure of Irish nationalist groups already well established and in control of the movement. Naïve about Ireland's own sectarianism and unable to gain the support of the Catholic Committee, Shelley left Dublin defeated.

From this point, Shelley's political activism shifted from direct political involvement to writing politically reformist poetry.[10] He wrote to Godwin on March 18, 1812, "I submit I shall address myself no more to the illiterate, I will look to events which it will be impossible that I can share, and make myself the cause of an effect which will take place ages after I shall have moldered into dust."[11] Shelley's political philosophy turns from a focus on the present and the common masses to the future and the highly educated minority. He begins to regard reform as a complex and gradual process working its way down from the imaginations of the educated to the ranks of "the illiterate." Shelley changed his approach to encouraging reform from a more direct involvement—handing out political pamphlets to passersby on the streets of Dublin—to poetic influence—*writing* a future politics through aesthetic creation. Descending from his revolutionary soapbox, Shelley instead imagines his poetry as a vehicle to move reform forward. The change involves not only a change in his idea of poetry, but a change in his concept of history. Shelley's poetic politics grows into his philosophy of history as a "great poem" progressing and stagnating as the imaginations of people expand and contract. In Shelley's philosophy, history is not a series of events acting upon humankind but a human-constructed system of representation similar to the structure of poetry itself.

SHELLEY'S *Defence of Poetry*

Shelley crystallized his ideas on poetry, history, and politics in *A Defence of Poetry* in 1821 after his friend Thomas Love Peacock questioned the value of these in his essay *The Four Ages of Poetry*. In *The Four Ages*, Peacock divides literary history into four ages of iron, gold, silver, and brass, arguing that poetry is ineffectual in the present age of science and reason. Poetry, according to Peacock, attained perfection in the golden age of Homer by virtue of its novelty. "The maturity of poetry may be considered the infancy of history,"[12] since in early history no tradition had yet been established to which poetry must inevitably be compared. With the progress of history comes the decline of poetry, beginning with the silver age when "the sciences of morals and of mind advance towards perfection . . . [and] poetry can no longer accompany them in their progress" (*FA* 761). Poetry loses its influence in the face of prolific advances in philosophy and science, and because it must compete with the great poetry of the past. Science overtakes poetry as civilization matures beyond the need of "the ornamental":

> Poetry was the mental rattle that awakened the attention of intellect in the infancy of civil society: but for the maturity of mind to make a serious business of the playthings of its childhood, is as absurd as for a full-grown man to rub his gums with coral, and cry to be charmed to sleep by the jingle of silver bells. (*FA* 764)

Peacock's diminishing of poetry was a blow to Shelley's entire livelihood. Shelley's work, Peacock suggested, was child's play outdated by philosophy and science, and Shelley reacted passionately. Peacock's essay drove Shelley to "a sacred rage"[13] most likely because it unearthed Shelley's own fears about the substantive worth of his talent. Ironically, even as Shelley poured all of his energy into a politics of poetic invention, he had doubted the philosophical maturity of poetry. In 1819, he wrote to Peacock, "I consider Poetry very subordinate to moral and political science, and if I were well, certainly I should aspire to the latter; for I can conceive a great work, embodying the discoveries of all the ages and harmonizing the contending creeds by which mankind have been ruled."[14] Despite, or perhaps even because of, his own past conviction, Shelley of 1821 is indignant at his friend's suggestion that poetry is ineffectual, and he is no longer satisfied with laying claim to a vocation merely "subordinate to moral and political science." *A Defence of Poetry*, thus, is Shelley's attempt to fully convince *himself* as well as Peacock, that poetry is a crucial agent of political reform.

The conclusion of his argument in fact leads him to an even more ambitious prospect, however, since Shelley explodes his own dichotomy of poetry and political science, or "moral values" and "the real world," by redefining reciprocally, poetry as history and history as poetry. The *Defence* exposes Peacock's historical grid, and the whole tradition on which it is based, as a product of perception rather than an account of fact, one that is itself a form of poetry. Poetry, according to the *Defence*, is an innovation of language that mirrors and initiates the flux of time, while history is "that great poem," an amalgamation of poems written throughout history, actually precipitating that history in "the chaos of a cyclic poem." (*DP* 112) Reversing his own earlier opinion, Shelley eventually subordinated political science to poetry. Historicist and Marxist critics have described this turn to poetic praxis as an "aesthetic ideology," a veiled retreat from history or an illusory transcending of history, seeking finally to end history in an apocalyptic vision.[15] In contrast to this interpretation, Shelley's poetry and philosophy engage history by rethinking the very terms by which we understand history. Poetry does not seek an end to history. For Shelley, the transcendence or end of history would be no less than the absence of poetry altogether, since history itself is a poetic creation.

What might be seen as Shelley's turn away from politics toward aesthetic idealism is actually his turn away from the idealism of his youth to a more sophisticated understanding of politics and history as a system of language and signs. Mark Kipperman argues against the interpretation of Shelley as an idealist, arguing instead that Shelley "demands that utopia emerge within historical struggles."[16] What is perhaps more telling of Shelley's politics, however, is his redefining of "historical struggle" in terms of the structure of poetry. Once he understands history as "poiesis"—as human creation—it becomes unimportant to differentiate between a historical age's affecting poetry or poetry's affecting a historical age. The relationship between poetry and history, the ideal and the real, is not a dialectic for Shelley since he rejects the common understanding of history and poetry as oppositional. The two work in agreement, according to Shelley, by virtue of identification.

THE POLITICS OF AESTHETIC FORM

Shelley understands poetry in two different modes throughout his *Defence*: poetry, as he describes it, is specific written works in verse form—

Dante, Homer, Milton—and poetry is generally any imaginative invention—poets are "institutors of laws," "founders of civil society," "inventors of the arts," and "teachers" (*DP* 112). Metaphor is the tool of poetry as specific verse, imagination the tool of poetry as general invention. Both metaphor and imagination are forms of the spirit of innovation, and each points to knowledge as a system of interdependent perceptions (imagination) and expressions (metaphor). Imagination, as the innovation of perceptions, creates metaphor, the innovation of expressions. New expressions in turn create new perceptions, forming the cycle of change that we understand as history. History is thus made up of the components of imagination and metaphor.

Shelley first defines imagination by differentiating it from the faculty of reason. Reason, he says, is the principle of analysis, imagination that of synthesis. Reason is the faculty of *knowing* the world, while imagination is the faculty of *interpreting* the world by understanding the relations of things. Imagination, in this most general sense, is the recognition of our system of interpretive signs: "men, even in the infancy of society, observe a certain order in their words and actions, distinct from that of the objects and the impressions represented by them" (*DP* 110). This observation of order distinct from objects drives our system of signs, our expressions of imagination. This expression of interpretation (of imagination) is the metaphor, or figurative language, of poetry. Poetry celebrates not objects themselves, but how we represent the objective world to ourselves. It recognizes "the good which exists in the relation subsisting first between existence and perception, and secondly between perception and expression" (*DP* 111–112). All knowledge is dependent on this indeterminate system of perception and expression, and the innovation of the system is poetry. Indeed, according to Shelley, this innovative interpretation is the key to poetry's reformist politics. Poetry's political energy arises from its focus on perception and expresstion, on the subjective, as opposed to the objective, world. Poetry holds the potential for spurring progressive change because it is a system of fluid interpretation and expression distinct from the fixed object it represents. In Shelley's philosophy, poetry is the spirit of active reform because it is through changing signs that we change our perceptions, leading to a change in future signs, expressions, and institutions.

The spirit of poetry—that is, the invention and manipulation of our system of signs—pervades all existence and determines all knowledge since "all things exist as they are perceived; at least in relation to the percipient" (*DP* 137). Shelley understands reality as inevitably filtered through our images of things, the most important expression of which is language. Following Rousseau's theory of the "originarily metaphoric,"[17] Shelley contends, "[i]n the infancy of society, every author is necessarily a poet, because language itself is poetry" (*DP* 111). At its inception, language is a new and innovative means of interpreting the world. As language becomes standard usage, poetry becomes the innovation of these standards. Poetry, as creative verse, invents new language through the use of metaphor:

> [A Poet's] language is vitally metaphorical; that is, it marks the before unapprehended relations of things and perpetuates their apprehension, until the words which represent them become, through time, signs for portions or classes of thought instead of pictures of integral thoughts; and then, if no new poets should arise to create afresh the associations which have been thus disorganized, language will be dead to all the nobler purposes of human intercourse. (*DP* 111)

Poetry is the flux of language, perpetuating apprehension by holding the potential for new and continuously proliferating interpretations. Poetry's meaning is far from that first intended by the poet: poetry offers a continuum of new relationships, new understanding. Jerrold Hogle observes: "The only manifestly constant principle [in Shelley's poetic theory] . . . is the vague potentiality that all words carry forward, their tendency to extend themselves beyond themselves to other locations." These locations are less spatial than temporal, since it is by the "different needs of interpretation at different points in time" that poetry is "transfigured."[18]

According to Shelley, poetry and the imagination are open to innovation in ways which objective fact can never be: "Time, which destroys the beauty and the use of the story of particular facts, stripped of the poetry which should invest them, augments that of poetry, and forever develops new and wonderful applications of the eternal truth which it contains" (*DP* 115). Poetry's "eternity" or "truth content" can best be understood as eternal change. This innovation is the burden of every new poet as well as every new literary critic. "Every great poet," says Shelley, "must inevitably innovate upon the example of his predecessors in the exact structure of his peculiar versification" (*DP* 114). Poetry begets poetry, gathering "a sort of reduplication" from its readers and interpreters.

Unlike reason, or "the story of particular facts," which attempts to determine a final truth, indeterminacy is the very essence of the poetical. Factual understanding is finite, while "all high poetry is infinite. . . . Veil after veil may be undrawn, and the inmost naked beauty of the meaning never exposed" (*DP* 131). Poetry paradoxically "strips the veil of familiarity from the world" and "spreads its own figured curtain" (*DP* 137). It unveils the system of representation that pervades our existence by ironically magnifying the figural nature of language and by multiplying language's veils. Since interpretation never reaches its final point, poetry inspires infinite creation, and thus always points to the future. Poets are called prophets, says Shelley, not simply because they see the future, but because they are the seeds for future change: the poet "beholds the future in the present, and his thoughts are the germs of the flowers and fruit of latest time" (*DP* 112).

Poetry is a historical as well as political force by virtue of its opposition to rules of conventional language, to the systems of knowledge of the present and the past. "Versification for Shelley is a radical kind of violence carried out against the past."[19] Poetry, Shelley argues, is a mirror "of the gigantic shadows which futurity casts upon the present" (*DP* 140). Future's shadows become realizations through poetic expression, and this precisely is the spirit of historical change. Shelley prefigures Theodor Adorno who has similarly argued that "in a subtle sense reality ought to imitate art works, not the other way around. By their presence, art works signal the possibility of the non-existent; their reality testifies to the feasibility of the unreal, the possible."[20] Aesthetic "unreality" embodies the unreality of the future. Thus, "future is contained within the present" (*DP* 110). Poetry writes the future into being by rewriting perceptions of the past and by radically changing perceptions of the present.

Poetic Politics in "Ode to the West Wind"

Shelley's encomium to the forces of nature in "Ode to the West Wind" (1819) illustrates his temporal conception of poetic politics in *Defence of Poetry*. The wind, in the "Ode," is a figure of nature that Shelley longs to emulate; it is a metaphor for poetry itself, yet it is distinctly a figure of motion, especially temporal since the west wind is the force of the changing cycles of the seasons:

O wild West Wind, thou breath of Autumn's being,
Thou, from whose unseen presence the leaves dead
Are driven, like ghosts from an enchanter fleeing,

Yellow, and black, and pale, and hectic red,
Pestilence-stricken multitudes: O thou,
Who chariotest to their dark wintry bed

The winged seeds, where they lie cold and low,
Each like a corpse within its grave, until
Thine azure sister of the Spring shall blow

Her clarion o'er the dreaming earth, and fill
(Driving sweet buds like flocks to feed in air)
With living hues and odours plain and hill:

Wild Spirit, which art moving everywhere;
Destroyer and preserver; hear, oh, hear!

Poetry, like the wind, is transformative movement, change; it is the break from the past in the coming of the future, figured in the poem as, respectively, winter and spring, for it is the future to which Shelley now looks for the blossoming of political reform. For Shelley, poetic nature, blowing "Her clarion o'er the dreaming earth," is the spirit of political revolution: politics in the image of this resurrection is one of continual reform generating freedom through imagination, figured by the freedom of movement in the "winged seeds."

Shelley's nexus of temporal flux and political freedom is inspired by William Godwin's political philosophy of stasis and flux, two opposing tendencies of political order. To remain static, Godwin argues, is to conserve the social order, while to progress is to challenge the status quo and thus to ensure the exercise of free will. Godwin explains stasis as the natural impulse of government, and progress as the natural impulse of the individual imagination. While "one of the most unquestionable characteristics of the human mind" is its "progressive nature," Godwin writes, "it is the express tendency of positive institution to retain that with which it is conversant for ever in the same state."[21] It is this conflict between governmental stasis and individual imaginative desire for progress that causes rebellion. Godwin ultimately recommends a state free from government—that is free of the desire for stasis—since it is only under such a state that the natural progression of the mind is unfettered, and the violence of rebellion quelled. In light of Godwin's "philosophical anarchism,"[22] Shelley's figuring of poetry as seasonal change is a figuring of poetry as political freedom, and both political freedom and poetry are joined under Shelley's greater figure of change, history as poetry itself. Poetry is the central driving force of time and change, the proper course of which is the emancipation of humankind. In the closing of "Ode to the West Wind," poetry and the progression of time merge as Shelley the poet longs for the power to precipitate spring (a figure for future political freedom):

> Drive my dead thoughts over the universe
> Like withered leaves to quicken a new birth!
> And, by the incantation of this verse,
>
> Scatter, as from an unextinguished hearth
> Ashes and sparks, my words among mankind!
> Be through my lips to unawakened earth
>
> The trumpet of a prophecy! O, Wind,
> If Winter comes, can Spring be far behind?

Thoughts themselves become the seeds driven by the wind, now represented as "the incantation of this verse." The language of poetry becomes the "seeds," the temporal force of nature driving winter into spring, past into future, and awakening the sleep of oppression into the resurrection of freedom. Working against a conservative government's tendency to remain "forever in the same state," poetry—as the embodiment of change—is the principle of progressive politics and the force which drives time forward.

Following the poetic vocation described in "Ode to the West Wind," *A Defence of Poetry* politicizes verse by locating its historical force in the form of poetry itself, rather than in its content.[23] Poetry is not relevant to history or politics by virtue of its making reference to, or of its reflecting in content, the politics of its day. Classical poetry, according to Shelley, is "poetic truth" because it does not merely find relevance in its historical context or through the moral standards of its day. By virtue of its aesthetic form, the poetry of Homer and Virgil is historical *process* rather than historical moment. As Bruce Haley notes, Shelley "contextualizes the work in its future as much as in its present or past, refusing to limit its 'history' to its genesis or its immediate influence on society or poetry."[24] Poetry can be judged only by its ability to change meaning over time, and thus by its ability to create, rather than reflect, truth.

The Poetry of History

Shelley's understanding of history as poetic change through interpretation (and likewise his understanding of poetry as historical progression) emerges in the *Defence* from his description of history as a system of signs similar to language. Shelley describes our linear timeline as "grammatical forms which express the moods of time" (*DP* 114). These forms of time are necessary to order our temporal existence, just as the grammar of language is necessary for communication. Both are tools that simultaneously govern and obey our perceptions. History thus is bound with language. Humankind begins to have a concept of history—of past, present, and future—only when we have a language to describe it. As the language that controls our conceptions of time and our perceptions of change over time, history is a poetic, potentially innovative, system of signs. If our entire order of reality is a grammatical form, Shelley suggests, we have a hand in creating and changing our reality. As Greg Kucich remarks, "Shelley was aware all along of the importance of fashioning a 'usable past' rather than being controlled by, as he puts is, the 'slow victory of the spirit of the past over that of the present.'"[25] History, to Shelley, is our most sophisticated system of representative language; it is "that great poem which all poets, like the co-operating thoughts of one great mind, have built up since the beginning of the world" (*DP* 124). This history-as-poem is not linear; we cannot trace a straight path from past oppression to present or future freedom, nor can we determine any clear historical cause and effect in terms of a fixed past causing a fixed present or future. Neither the past, the present, nor the future are static or fixed: each is formed and reformed by perceptions and expressions that are *created by* context and that *create* that context. Rather than a line of progression, this is a "rhythm" of history, a continuous, but unpredictable, pattern of change.

As Shelley begins to figure history as poetry, a clear reciprocity between poetry and time emerges. The poet writes time and time writes poetry: individual poems "are episodes of that cyclic poem written by time upon the memories of men" (*DP* 125). Initially asserting that poets are revolutionary because, by writing, they precipitate historical change, Shelley also contends that revolution occurs also when history "writes" innovative verse:

> All the authors of revolutions in opinion are not only necessarily poets as they are inventors, nor even as their words unveil the permanent analogy of things by images which participate in the life of truth; but *as their periods are harmonious and rhythmical, and contain in themselves the elements of verse*; being the echo of the eternal music. (*DP* 115; *my emphasis*)

Containing "the elements of verse," revolutionary moments in history are periods of increased political indeterminacy, moments open to a surge in innovative conceptions of government. Revolutionary politics reinterprets the past, as poetry reinterprets language, in order to revise government in the present. This vital creativity renders revolution the greatest poem of history.

While poets govern, in the most general sense, our very understanding of reality, they remain "unacknowledged" because we take for granted "the permanent analogy of things by images" (*DP* 115). Poets' acknowledgment would more likely come in the negative, in a world without poetry, without regenerative time: in an imagined end of history itself. The possibility of the end of poetry/history has been shown, Shelley suggests, in past epochs that have neared poetic stasis. After the fall of the Roman empire, Shelley explains, "the world would have fallen into utter anarchy and darkness, but that there were found poets among the authors of Christian and chivalric systems of manners and religion" (*DP* 125). Time itself seems nearly dormant during this near "extinction of the poetic principle." History-as-poetry then awakens in the Renaissance with a burst of artistic genius as an "invisible wind, nourishing its everlasting course with strength and swiftness" (*DP* 126). Shelley reminds us, however, that the threat of poetic extinction remains in the "recurrence of impressions blunted by reiteration" (*DP* 137). The cyclic poem of time cannot move without the momentum of individual invention. Without poetic innovation there is, on one level, no history known to us. We conceive of historical epochs (the golden age of poetry in Peacock's essay, for instance) according to social, artistic, and political change. Without poetry—without these changes and without the tools to interpret them—the past would be essentially one homogenous void.

Political oppression indeed thrives on such homogeneity. For Shelley, periods of political oppression are poetically dead, morally corrupt, and temporally static. In an image reminiscent of the fertile "winged seeds" in "Ode to the West Wind," Shelley argues that poetry, "if blighted, denies the fruit and the seed, and withholds from the barren world the nourishments and the succession of the scions of the tree of life" (*DP* 135). The most basic nourishment, Shelley explains, is the "sensibility to pleasure" experienced in aesthetic perception and appreciation. As a "sensibility" also to political reform, it is the target of social corruption:

> For the end of social corruption is to destroy all sensibility to pleasure. . . . It begins at the imagination and the intellect as at the core, and distributes itself thence as a paralyzing venom through the affection into the very appetites until all become a torpid mass in which hardly sense survives. (*DP* 123–124)

Time, the poet, and the citizen are inextricably linked in a circular chain of interdependence: the denial of political freedom is the paralysis of the imagination which finally is the paralysis of time itself. With no ability to write or read the eternal vision of poetry there is no ability to write social innovation. Shelley's *Defence of Poetry* reaches its final claim: the blighting of poetry is no less than the end of history itself.

In this analogy, Shelley finally accomplishes, although in a very different capacity, what he set out to do a decade before in Ireland. He reinvents politics by redefining traditional conceptions of the relationship between poetry and history. We cannot judge poetry, he argues, according to its effect on an external historical event since history is itself a form of poetry, made up of perception and expression. Proclaiming the formative dimension of interpretation and representation, Shelley's history-as-poetry suggests the postmodern conviction that "political power [is] a text that you can read,"[26] a conception that has profoundly liberating and reformist potential since individuals can reinterpret and rewrite this text. Thus, poetry's "open-ended character becomes the source of greater activism."[27] For when we understand the pervasive power of perception and expression, we can control and manipulate that power: "poetry," says Shelley, "defeats the curse which binds us to be subjected to the accident of surrounding impressions" (*DP* 137). Understood as poetic perception and expression, history is an indeterminate progression, a conception that renders the past, present, and future as malleable representations for political and social invention.

Notes

1. *The Works of P. B. Shelley* (Hertfordshire: Wordsworth Editions, Ltd., 1994), 159–161.

2. *A Defence of Poetry* (*The Complete Works of Percy Bysshe Shelley*, Vol VII, ed. Roger Ingpen [New York: Gordian Press, 1964]. Hereafter cited within the text by *DP* and page number.) points to Hayden White's interpretation of historical works in *Metahistory: The Historical Imagination in Nineteenth Century Europe* (Baltimore: Johns Hopkins University Press, 1973), which explains historical writing not as the unmediated communication of fact, but as the "invention" of the historian. White thus examines the formalist qualities of historical writing utilizing those terms most applied to fiction: "emplotment," "comedy," "tragedy," "romance." Shelley's argument mirrors White's and provides an example of it: Shelley's construction of history as poetic narrative is a metanarrative: it is his own narrative construction of history.

3. Shelley published two pamphlets in support of the independence of Ireland: *An Address to the Irish People* and *Proposals for an Association of Philanthropists*. He also spoke before the Catholic Committee at the Fishamble Street meeting on February 28. See Richard Holmes, *Shelley: the Pursuit* (London: Weidenfeld and Nicolson, 1974), chapter 5, for a full account of Shelley's campaign in Ireland in 1812.

4. Shelley to James Hogg, April 1811, quoted in P. M. S. Dawson, *The Unacknowledged Legislator: Shelley and Politics* (Oxford: Clarendon Press, 1980), 77.

5. Dawson, 80.

6. Kenneth Neil Cameron, *The Young Shelley: Genesis of a Radical* (New York: Collier, 1950), 172.

7. Shelley writes in his Preface to *The Revolt of Islam*, for instance: "The revulsion occasioned by the atrocities of the demagogues and the re-establishment of successive tyrannies in France was terrible, and felt in the remotest corner of the civilized world. Could they listen to the plea of reason who had groaned under the calamities of a social state, according to the provisions of which, one man riots in luxury whilst another famishes for want of bread? Can he who the day before was a trampled slave, suddenly become liberal-minded, forbearing and independent?" (*The Works of P.B. Shelley*, 1994, 50).

8. Percy Bysshe Shelley, *A Philosophical View of Reform*, ed. T.W. Rolleston (London: Oxford University Press, 1920), 89.

9. 8 March 1812, *Letters of Percy Bysshe Shelley*, ed. Fredrick Jones (Oxford: Clarendon Press, 1964), no. 173. Godwin, however, saw in Shelley's enthusiasm a repetition of the revolutionists' mistakes. He wrote back to Shelley on 14 March, "But so reasoned the French Revolutionists. Auspicious and admirable

materials were working in the general mind of France; but these men said, as you say, when we look on the last twenty years, we are seized with a sort of moral skepticism, 'we must own we are eager that something should be done.' And see what has been the result of their doings!" Godwin's condemnation of Shelley's political actions in Ireland, along with the resistance Shelley met among the Irish themselves, finally convinced him to give up his political work there.

10. See, for instance, of Shelley's major works, *The Revolt of Islam* (1817), *Prometheus Unbound* (1820), and *Hellas* (1821).

11. *Letters*, no. 176.

12. *The Four Ages of Poetry* in *English Romantic Writers*, ed. David Perkins (New York: Harcourt, Brace, Jovanovich, 1967), 760. Hereafter cited within the text by *FA* and page number.

13. *Letters*, no. 605.

14. *Letters*, no. 491.

15. In *Unbuilding Jerusalem: Apocalypse and Romantic Representation* (Ithaca: Cornell University Press, 1993), Steven Goldsmith cites Friedrich Schiller's *On The Aesthetic Education of Man* as an example of apocalyptic writing that describes aesthetics as beyond the reach of historical change. In Schiller's essay, Goldsmith contends, "[s]uffering ends in the freedom provided by the aesthetic, and that freedom is literally, almost reductively, apocalyptic in that it means *freedom from history*" (7). See also Jerome McGann, *The Romantic Ideology* (Chicago: University of Chicago Press, 1983) and Terry Eagleton, *The Ideology of the Aesthetic* (Oxford: Basil Blackwell, 1990).

16. "History and Ideality: the Politics of Shelley's *Hellas*," *Studies in Romanticism* 30 (Summer 1991): 167. Kipperman, like myself, takes issue with Jermone McGann who criticizes Shelley's "idealist escapism" as "a reflex against the despair of facing up to history" (150).

17. In *Of Grammatology* (Baltimore: Johns Hopkins University Press, 1974), Jacques Derrida uses this phrase to describe Rousseau's theory that language is by its essence metaphorical. Derrida quotes Rousseau's *Essay on the Origin of Language*: "As man's first motives for speaking were of the passions [and not of needs], his first expressions were tropes. Figurative language was the first to be born" (105–6).

18. *Shelley's Process: Radical Transfiguration and the Development of His Major Works* (New York: Oxford University Press, 1988), 4.

19. Paul Fry, "Shelley's Defence of Poetry in Our Time," in *Modern Critical Views: Percy Bysshe Shelley*, ed. Harold Bloom (New York: Chelsea House, 1985), 182.

20. Theodor Adorno, *Aesthetic Theory* (London: Routledge and Kegan Paul, 1984), 192.

21. *Enquiry Concerning Political Justice*, quoted in Michael Henry Scrivener, *Radical Shelley: The Philosophical Anarchism and Utopian thought of Percy Bysshe Shelley* (Princeton: Princeton University Press, 1982), 11–12.

22. P. M. S. Dawson uses this phrase to title his chapter on Godwin's political theory and its influence on Shelley. Godwin's *Enquiry Concerning Political Justice* rejects government in favor of independent individual authority. Dawson explains, "For Godwin freedom is not just one good among others, to be balanced against them until a satisfactory compromise is arrived at, as it is for Paine; it is an inescapable duty. . . . Man's responsibility to truth and morality imposes on him the necessity of preserving his independence against all outside authorities that claim the right to determine his actions" (87).

23. Poetry that tries, in its content, to affect politics or that embodies the poet's personal conception of right and wrong is not poetry at all, Shelley argues, but a corruption of the form. Shelley insists, "[t]he period in our history of the grossest degradation of drama is the reign of Charles II, when all forms in which poetry had been accustomed to be expressed became hymns to the triumph of kingly power over liberty and virtue" (*DP* 122).

24. "Shelley, Peacock, and the Reading of History" *Studies in Romanticism* 39 (Fall 1990): 461.

25. "Eternity and the Ruins of Time: Shelley and the Construction of Cultural History" in *Shelley: Poet and Legislator of the World,* eds. Betty T. Bennet and Stuart Curran (Baltimore: The Johns Hopkins University Press, 1996), 16.

26. Fredric Jameson, *Postmodernism, or, the Cultural Logic of Late Capitalism* (Durham: Duke University Press, 1991), 186.

27. Ernesto Laclau, "Politics and the Limits of Modernity," in *Universal Abandon?: the Politics of Postmodernism*, ed. Andrew Ross (Minneapolis: University of Minnesota Press, 1988), 79.

CHAPTER FOUR

Painting out the Past

Jacques-Louis David's Attempt to Begin History Again

Stephen Brown

There was a moment when the painter Jacques-Louis David came close to a total redefinition of the role of the artist. It occurred in the final hours of Robespierre's reign. In the Assembly, as the tide was visibly turning against the great terrorist and he seemed to have lost the energy to stand against it, David called out across the floor to him, "I will drink the hemlock with you, Robespierre!"

Well, it was easy enough to drink the hemlock in those days. All David needed to do in order to follow his leader to the guillotine was to continue to defend him. He chose not to, of course, and, although it was a near thing, managed thus to save his own skin.

Had he sacrificed himself to the pure vision of the Republic that he had shared with Robespierre, he would have set a new standard for the artist *engagée.* That he did not, and instead went on to paint in the service of Napoleon and the Empire, has made him seem an opportunist and has discredited the strength of his political vision and its relationship to his art. This may or may not be unfair to David, but it is certainly unfair to his paintings of the Revolutionary and pre-Revolutionary periods. These are works that fuse aesthetic and political visions. As revolutionary works, they attack not just the state but the premises of the state, and, as I will try to show, its very history.

When, after Ropespierre had fallen, David was imprisoned and his own life hung in the balance, one of the factors that weighed against him was his vote for the execution of the King eighteen months previous; not just the fact of the vote, but the sheer ingratitude it represented. For David had been the recipient of much royal patronage. To see how a state could get itself into the position of funding works that attacked it, we have to look back about thirty-five years before the *The Oath of the Horatii,* when state patronage in France began a fundamental shift.

The shift can be traced back to the watershed year of 1750, the year when Rousseau, suffering from heat-stroke, paused beneath an oak tree, and had revealed to him his vocation as a writer. The bit of prose that convinced him of his own genius (and would shortly begin to convince others) was the kernel of his prize-winning essay on the topic of "Whether the restoration of the Sciences and Arts has contributed to the purification of morals." This is the *prosopopoeia*, the address he puts in the mouth of the ancient Roman hero Fabricius:

> "Gods!" you would have said, "what has become of the thatch roofs and the rustic hearths where moderation and virtue used to dwell? What fatal splendor has replaced Roman simplicity? What is this alien speech? What are these effeminate morals? What is the meaning of these statues, these Paintings, these buildings? Fools, what have you done? You, the Masters of Nations, made yourselves the slaves of the frivolous men you vanquished? Do Rhetoricians govern you? Was it in order to enrich Architects, Painters, Sculptors, and Thespians that you spilled your blood in Greece and in Asia? Have the spoils of Carthage become the prey of a flute-player? Romans, hasten to overturn these Amphitheaters; smash these marbles; burn these paintings; drive out these slaves who subjugate you and whose fatal arts corrupt you. Let other hands acquire fame for vain talents; the only talent worthy of Rome is that of conquering the world and making virtue reign in it . . .[1]

Later, he offers an even more explicit critique of contemporary art ("aberrations of the heart and reason") and goes on to admit that the royal academies could play a positive role in the promotion of virtue by award-

FIG. 4.1 Boucher, *Leda and the Swan* (1741); The Swedish National Art Museums

ing prizes to works which would "revive the love of virtue in Citizens' hearts."[2]

In making these arguments, Rousseau (deftly using a rhetorical device to argue against a culture that has allowed tself to be governed by "Rhetoricians") recommends exactly the kind of moralizing, instructive history he has himself just constructed in the *prosopopoeia*. His suggestions were not immediately adopted. Madame Pompadour, Louis XV's favorite, remained a powerful presence at court. She had succeeded in placing her uncle, Charles de Tournehem (who may actually have been her father), in the position of *Directeur Général de Bâtiments*, where he became the kingdom's most powerful dispenser of art patronage. Pompadour's favorite painter was Boucher, and his canvases are indeed filled with the "aberrations of reason" taken from ancient mythology that Rousseau complained so bitterly about. They are the very images of sensual pleasure least likely to contribute to that Spartan discipline Rousseau yearned for [fig. 4.1].

FIG. 4.2 Jacques-Louis David, *The Death of Seneca* (1773); Musée du Petit Palais, © © Photothèque des Musées de la Ville de Paris

The accession of Louis XVI accelerated the process of change. His appointee as *Directeur de Bâtiments* was the Comte d'Angiviller, a man who took Rousseau's advice to heart.

> In December 1774, three months after assuming the office . . . , Comte d'Angiviller informed the Royal Academy of the king's intention to '*ranimer la vertu et les sentiments patriotiques*' through a set of moralizing history paintings drawn from ancient and French history and statues of great French men (no women were included), to be commissioned every other year. Four statues and eight to ten paintings were ordered for each biennial exhibition of the Academy's works, held in the Salon carré of the Louvre beginning in 1777. Taken together this series of paintings and sculptures constitutes one of the most ambitious and sustained programmes of state patronage in the history of French art.[3]

Rousseau was not the only critic urging a new tone in the paintings of the time; his friend Diderot (whom he was on his way to visit when struck with his revelation) was a more perceptive and profound art critic.[4] But d'Angiviller's commissions of 1776 include a scene that seems to refer back to Rousseau's prize essay: he asked for an "Example of disinterestedness among the Romans: Fabricius refusing the presents of the ambassadors of Pyrrus." The other set themes of that year indicate further the sort of moralizing tone d'Angiviller favored: "Example of the encouragement of work among the Romans: Cressinus displaying his agricultural implements. . . . Example of heroic resolution among the Romans: Portia proving to her husband Brutus that she has the courage to kill herself if the plot against Caesar fails."[5] This is exactly what Rousseau was hoping for: the Academy setting moralizing standards for its prizes, and doing so within a framework of Roman Republican virtue.

Born in 1748, David was only two years old when Rousseau wrote his essay, but he was coming into his maturity at the time of d'Angiviller's

FIG. 4.3 Jacques-Louis David, *Antiochus and Stratonice* (1774); École Nationale Supérieure des Beaux-Arts, Paris

FIG. 4.4 Jacques-Louis David, *Belisarius Receiving Alms* (1781); Lille, Musée des Beaux-Arts, Paris,© Photo RMN

commissions. As a student of the French Academy, competing actively for its prizes, his development as an artist was intimately linked with the moralizing ideals d'Angiviller aimed to promulgate.

The academic prize for which David competed was the *Prix de Rome*; the opportunity to spend a year or more in Rome, at state expense, seeing ancient Roman and Italian Renaissance art at first hand, studying painting under French teachers with like-minded compatriots, with a near-guaranteed career back in Paris at the end of it. In order to win this plum, qualifying students submitted a work in the genre of "history-painting." A specified subject was set; the artist constructed a scene to illustrate it. But more than a simple image was involved—the artist had to find a way to convey the whole narrative through one pictured instant.

FIG. 4.5 Jacques-Louis David, *Andromache Mourning Hector* (1783); École Nationale Supérieure des Beaux-Arts, Paris

David's first major submission was in 1773, the last year of the reign of Louis XV.[6] The set subject was the *Death of Seneca* [fig. 4.2]. Again there is a connection to Rousseau's essay—the tyrant causing Seneca's death is the same Nero whom Rousseau has Fabricius despise as the "flute-player" in his diatribe. The following year's topic was *Antiochus and Stratonice* [fig. 4.3], in which the physician Erasistratus sees that the young prince Antiochus is wasting away with love for his father's, the king's, new wife, Stratonice. While in Rome, David completed a hand-me-down commission from his teacher, Vien, *St. Roch interceding for the plague-stricken*. On his return to Paris, he completed *Belisarius Receiving Alms* (1781) [fig. 4.4], in which a Roman soldier sees his old general reduced to beggary in the streets, and *Andromache*

FIG. 4.6 Jacques-Louis David, *Horatio Standing over the Body of his Sister* (1781); Graphische Sammlung Albertina, Wien

Mourning Hector (1783) [fig. 4.5]. With these paintings he gained full membership in the Academy and official recognition in the form of studio and lodgings in the Louvre. He was a success.

The paintings' narratives seem to conform to Rousseau's dicta, giving "not only agreeable enlightenment, but also salutary teachings."[7] They do this under royal patronage in a way that was entirely pleasing to the court. A tacit compromise had been arranged, whereby the public face of the monarchy changed from sensuality to moral improvement. The paintings represent virtue through the characters of the dead hero, the grieving wife, the stoic philosopher, the abstinent lover, the forsaken general. These are virtuous characters—but where is their virility? See the hollow husk of a hero; watch a warrior reduced to beggary; an old philosopher has the blood drained from his body; a young man is wasting away in self-imposed impotence. Impotence is the subtext of all these paintings.[8] None of the central figures has the power of action. This was the approved and acceptable neoclassical discourse in the waning years of the *ancien régime*: accept, give in, acquiesce—die if you must, just do it gracefully.

In 1785, the Academy's set subject for its Rome prize was again an episode from early Roman history. The battle between the three Horatii and the three Curiatii has ended with one survivor, the senior of the Horatii brothers, and one victor, the city of Rome. On his return home, the triumphant Horatio is greeted by his sister Camilla, grieving for her dead lover, one of the Curiatii. In the most memorable telling of the tale, Corneille's, she explodes with a raging invective against Rome, and Horatio kills her on the spot. Whatever did the Academy have in mind with this subject? What kind of moral instruction could this possibly convey? An insane patriotism? If you speak against your country, your relatives are allowed to murder you?

David was long past having to fulfill the Academy's requirements, but after sketching the set scene [fig. 4.6], he chose to paint a related one, the moment when the three brothers are sworn by their father to commit their lives to battle for their city, *The Oath of the Horatii*[9] [fig. 4.7]. It provides a striking contrast to David's other neoclassical paintings, and to the neoclassicism of other artists like his teacher Vien. It captures the moment that precedes the action, rather than, as was typical, the moment that follows it; it represents the

FIG. 4.7 Jacques-Louis David, *The Oath of Horatii* (1785); Paris, Louvre, © Photo RMN

arousal of passion, not all passion spent. With this painting, neoclassical style was revived and re-animated. Death, old age, suicide, acquiescence, and impotence were supplanted by an electric charge of energy and commitment.

In talking about Rousseau's first discourse, Virginia Swain says that "the power to overturn rhetoric and govern the world in one's own language ... is shown to be a fiction."[10] But is it? Isn't this the thrill of David's painting? That he has overturned rhetoric, and is now governing the world in his own language? Many historians of art have seen the moment of the painting of the *Horatii* as a crucial one, the crux of the departure from the art of the *ancien régime.* I want to examine the way some of these different commentators have looked at David's moment from the perspective of *their* moments. Each of them finds a way to narrate the painting, but each narrative method is contingent upon its author's contemporary situation.[11] I don't do this to assert the superiority of my own narrative; if anything, the effect would tend to be an opposite one: to assert the contingency of all such narratives. Which is not, I will try to show, the same as asserting them useless.

A resolutely Marxist interpretation was offered by David L. Dowd in 1948. In his view, the *Oath* "fuses the morality and philosophy of the bourgeoisie and a vital and powerful realism comprehensible to the masses. David . . . transformed neo-classicism from a fashion into a style and from a fad into a propaganda weapon of the new order." He "imbued his canvases with the . . . political and social reformist philosophy of the rising middle classes."[12] The reaction of "the masses" is described in the book's opening passage, taken from a radical revolutionary journal, the *Père Duchêne*:[13]

> One day, early in the French Revolution, a peasant stood fascinated before a picture hanging in the Louvre: Jacques-Louis David's *Oath of the Horatii* . . . he could clearly perceive the patriotic and revolutionary message of David's severe and simple work of art . . .

Robert Rosenblum, writing in 1967, saw the *Oath* as a tremendous event in the history of art, comparable in its revolutionary force to the one begun by Masaccio and Donatello. He called it a "proclamation of moral energy,"[14] but limited his definition of the painting's moral to an assertion of patriotism. Rosenblum's own energy is devoted to demonstrating the work's formal, abstract achievement.

> From the many suggestions of stylistic reform that were offered in France by Greuze, Vien, and Brenet or in England by West, Hamilton, and Dance, David at last crystallizes a definitive statement whose pictorial power, like its moral power, marks an irreparable cleavage between an old and a new world. In the context of these earlier paintings, the severity of David's style, like the severity of the oath, creates, as it were, a *tabula rasa* of a new epoch. The box space, with its rigidly plotted ground plane and rectilinear alignments, invests the preliminary reforms of the 1760's and 1770's with an all-pervasive intellectual control that recalls the perspective studies of the Quattrocento; and within the precise boundaries of this stage-like atrium, the figures firmly take their earthbound poses with a consonant sense of geometric predetermination.[15]

In other words, David's accomplishment is a literal realization, a reification of the process of art history. He alone sees what the next step should be, and takes it, gathering up all of the diverse reforming impulses and from them creating the synthesis that drives them to their logical conclusion. In this narrative, he is the agent of aesthetic evolution.[16]

In his 1984 *Tradition and Desire*, Norman Bryson says that "The *Oath* is an exact image of visuality for the subject living under patriarchy."[17] ("Visuality" for Bryson characterizes a particular culture's way of constructing the process of seeing.)[18] Bryson's is an essentially tragic view of the painting. The young men are trapped in their own image, victims of a world of signs, encased in the plane of their father's swords and his patriarchal vision. The key to their tragedy is what they have unwittingly become, characters incapable of individual action outside the figure their culture has constructed for them.[19] At the same time, Bryson recognizes David's wish to identify with the protagonists' heroism, a wish that defies the detachment of his own diagnosis. But the diagnosis remains Bryson's key. The "why" of David's painting is locked in this perception which demands utterance—a sudden understanding of the tragic nature of patriarchy.

For Thomas Crow, writing in 1985, the painting's political content rests in its style, which is in revolt against the mannered discourse of both the rococo and the conventional neoclassical. His shorthand for this is "the conflict between style and anti-style."[20] The whole mannered artistic discourse—"style"—had come to symbolize the court ethos of dissimulation, what was known, perversely, as "*honnêteté*." A painting whose composition was flat, awkward, obvious rather than subtle—"anti-style"—was the kind of plain speaking with which to oppose aristocratic eloquence. David's new style was made possible by an opening that, Crow asserts, was created out of the dialogue between the high art of the *salons* and the popular art of newspaper criticism: "David's art represents yet another instance in which the 'handling' of high-cultural materials by a broadly popular audience allowed an artist, who was attentive to that process, to push beyond the given limits of his genre and redefine its capacities."[21] Crow aligns David (stylistically, not personally) with radical pamphleteers like Jean-Louis Carra, Gorsas, Brissot, and Marat. This alignment does not, though, constitute a cause-and-effect relationship. To explain what spurred David to create revolutionary paintings, Crow supposes in David a certain fear of becoming *déclassé*. He imagines a David for whom the workmanlike attitudes of the Academy smack of the artisan rather than of art. "David, in choosing a career in painting, had taken what threatened to be a step downward from the status his family had achieved."[22] In opposing the academy, he was claiming for himself a more noble status. In other words, it was out of fear of sinking deeper within the middle class that David created works that were aligned with radical journalism.

As can be guessed from the way I have paraphrased their arguments, all of these contemporary art historians are themselves subject to contextual analysis. Dowd, for example, sees David through a lens provided by Marx, where social classes have historical roles and behaviors assigned to them. Less obviously, he sees David through a lens provided by Soviet art-commissars, the men who promoted the now-infamous style of Socialist Realism. This is, I believe, the source of Dowd's notion that art for the masses must be realistic.[23]

Rosenblum's version of history is also conditioned by the art of his day. During the 1950s and 1960s abstract art came to dominate establishment tastes and a historically based criticism was developed in its defense. We came to see art history as the process through which Monet was followed by Cézanne was followed by Picasso was followed by Jackson Pollock in an inevitable evolution in the direction of increasing abstraction. This is the background that allows Rosenblum to see David fulfilling certain formal potentials in the art of his predecessors.

In Bryson's case, I imagine that it is feminist criticism's heightened consciousness of gender issues that grants him his cold view of patriarchy, and contemporary literary critical techniques that give him his exquisite consciousness of the fragile subject in a world of signs. In particular, it is deconstructivist criticism that leads him to see that the painting somehow negates itself.

I share with Thomas Crow a way of seeing that I think belongs to the generation that went to college with the Beatles. We acquired not just a fondness for, but also a belief in the power of popular culture, often dignified in the sixties as the "counterculture," and we find its influence too often neglected in earlier histories; we like finding historical precedent for the influence of popular culture on high art.

It may seem that I am indulging here in what has become a fashionable academic game, the game of "I can get outside your narrative before you can get outside mine." In this game, we attack our opponents' points of view by showing how they are conditioned by ideology, culture, period, gender, class. But it is not my intention to attack any of the historians I have discussed. I only want to indicate that they tell their own stories, write their own autobiographies, view what their backgrounds and cultures and experiences have made visible to them. In this they are like David.

To whom I now return, with the aim of using this very sense of contingency as a starting point for reaching an understanding of his crucial moment. The vision his painting reflects is very similar to the one Rousseau promotes in his *prosopopoeia*. The opening words of that statement championed virtue, moderation, simplicity, and the Roman, and railed against effeminacy and the sensual in art. They explicitly asked for a warrior culture and implicitly for a male, public definition of virtue. All of this is present as well in the *Horatii*, and it seems fair to assume that these ideas were very much present among the artists, intellectuals, and educated patrons with whom David associated in the 1780s. The difference between Rousseau's statement and David's is in the kind of rhetoric used. The reason Swain sees Rousseau's discourse as ultimately self-defeating is because it uses the very sort of rhetorical device that—it claims—is corrupting society.[24] David, as Crow and others have pointed out, uses a new rhetoric—a kind of primitivism, an anti-style with which to counter style. This is what is stunningly new about the painting, and I think that another difference may indicate its source. That difference is the sense of *beginning*. Rousseau's *prosopopoeia*, like the various paintings sponsored by d'Angiviller, and like David's earlier history paintings, is a rear-guard movement, defensive, critical, essentially despairing of the possibility of any action but a destructive or self-destructive one.

The fact that David invents, deliberately and self-consciously, a scene of beginning, of construction, energy, optimism, and the (literal) *avant-garde*,[25] indicates to me that this sense of possibility had to exist in David's world, that it was part of David's life and time to see that things need not go on as they had gone on before, but could be suddenly and radically changed. His previous work becomes an aria from a Handel opera, Cleopatra singing, "I weep for my fate . . ." and his present like the moment from *Messiah* where the prophet sings, "We might all be changed, in a moment, in the twinkling of an eye..." This is the realization that made the painting possible, and revolution too—the realization that a "Machiavellian moment" had occurred, an instant when "virtue" no longer appeared to apply to anything in the dominant culture, an instant of disorientation which he was able to seize in order to install his own rhetoric and his own definitions. I don't think that David had any specific political ideas in his head in 1785—he was not turning the academic cannons around to fire on the king; he was turning them around to fire on the past. After a career of history painting, he made a history painting that saw the possibility of *destroying* history, of going back before history to start history all over again. This is the vision that would eventually allow the revolutionaries to call 1792 the "Year One."

History painting and the history of painting are both, then, poetry. But if history is poetry, is it therefore useless?[26] No. That history is poetry simply allows us to read it in a different way—not as a "straightforward" recounting of facts but as evidence of how its culture (that is, the culture that produced it) thought, worked, and perceived. A document of written history is the crystallization of an instant in an ongoing dialogue between a culture and its past. Modern art historians writing about David, and David, painting out the immediate past to start over with a Roman one, and we ourselves, talking about them both, are all participants in this densely woven, ongoing, inescapable discourse.

Notes

1. Jean-Jacques Rousseau, *The First and Second Discourses*, trans. Victor Gourevitch (New York: Harper and Row, 1990), 12.

2. Rousseau, 23.

3. Andrew McClellan, "D'Angiviller's 'Great men' of France and the Politics of the Parlements," *Art History* 13, 2 (June 1990): 175–192, 175.

4. La Font de Saint-Yenne was another influential critic championing didactic, anti-rococo painting.

5. Hugh Honour, *Neo-Classicism* (Harmondsworth: Penguin, 1968), 82.

6. He had failed to complete his submission for the previous year, for which the subject had been Apollo and Diana attacking the children of Niobe, a subject that seems more Baroque in its messy violence than either rococo or neoclassical.

7. Rousseau, 23.

8. Although "sur-text" might be a better word, since powerlessness is visible on the most obvious level of viewing, the level that precedes any knowledge of the works' narrative basis.

9. Art historians, who are demon source trackers, have puzzled over this subject for generations, since David has chosen a scene that does not actually occur in any of the ancient or modern sources.

10. Virginia E. Swain, "Autobiographical Acts," in Dennis Hollier, *A New History of French Literature* (Cambridge: Harvard University Press, 1989), 548.

11. In general, it is Anglo-American art historians who see the moment as a crucial one; French art historians are content to criticize the hypotheses that attempt to explain the moment's significance, rarely offering their own.

12. D.L. Dowd, *Pageant Master of the Republic: Jacques-Louis David and the French Revolution* (Lincoln: University of Nebraska Press, 1948), 5–6.

13. The *Père Duchêne* article dates not from 1785 when the painting was first exhibited but from 1791.

14. Robert Rosenblum, *Transformations in Late Eighteenth Century Art* (Princeton: Princeton University Press, 1967), 70.

15. Rosenblum, 71–72.

16. In a previous work, *The International Style of 1800: A Study in Linear Abstraction,* Rosenblum said that "The *Horatii*, indeed, sums up the discoveries of these years and presents them in terms of a rigorous analysis of the problems of picture-making." This makes David into even more of an art historian or theorist.

17. Norman Bryson, *Tradition and Desire* (Cambridge: Cambridge University Press, 1984), 70.

18. In his own words, visuality is "the construction of vision under conditions of society and discourse."

19. They are—to take Bryson's argument farther than he does—double synecdoches. In their role as symbolic warriors they are the parts that stand for the whole; in their rigid masculinities, they are wholes that stand for a part.

20. Thomas Crow, *Painters and Public Life in Eighteenth Century Paris* (New Haven: Yale University Press, 1985), 223.

21. Crow, 254.

22. Crow, 231.

23. It is unlikely that French peasants had actually developed a taste for realism. The Soviet version of "socialist realism" is derived from Second Empire academicism.

24. ". . . the 'prosopopoeia' does more than represent writing's nefarious effects; it enacts them" (Swain, 548).

25. The three Horatii are pulled from the main troop of the Roman army to fight as a representative vanguard.

26. "For poetry makes nothing happen: it survives/In the valley of its saying where executives/Would never want to tamper; it flows south/From ranches of isolation and the busy griefs,/Raw towns that we believe and die in; it survives,/A way of happening, a mouth."—Auden

CHAPTER FIVE

The Power of "Kulturgeschichte"

100 Years in the House that Jacob Built: The Italian Renaissance

Carole Collier Frick

Introduction

I myself, as a modern fin-de-siècle historian of Renaissance Florence, live a thoroughly contemporary life replete with computers, microwave, and CDs thumping, in a big nineteenth-century house, in a small college town somewhere in the Midwest. I accommodate this well-built, vintage-1890 abode to the life demands of the present; with certain adaptations such as air conditioning, TV, modern plumbing, and cable, I do just fine. My field of scholarly endeavor likewise has been housed, up until a few decades ago, in an even older, vintage-1860 abode, built by a Swiss historian whose poetic architecture was so strong as to direct the agenda of Renaissance studies for at least one hundred years. While the vision of the Renaissance that Jacob Burckhardt first articulated in his 1860 classic, *Civilization of the Renaissance in Italy*, has now been eclipsed, one can hardly deny that his sweeping conception of the late medieval period in Italy, beginning with Dante and Petrarch, and ending in the mid-sixteenth century of Titian, has successfully stimulated modern interest in and study of this time and place called the Renaissance, where many have agreed that it was here the consciousness of modern man was born.[1]

In Burckhardt's house, the grand palazzo of the mind that he constructed, where he first ushered students and scholars alike into the great courtyard and public rooms to marvel at the frescoes and drink in the conversation (or vice versa), we historians of the twentieth century have also had to seek an adaptation. His portrait of the age, what he himself saw, was taken up in the United States by generations of historians in the twentieth century who then amended the discussion begun by him, and took it in other directions, revising some basic conclusions about the genesis of individualism, rejecting others, and adding things in areas of concern that Burckhardt had not covered. They also refocused Renaissance scholarship, not entirely but primarily, on the city of Florence. As late as the 1960s, scholars took their areas of research from suggestions and comments made by Burckhardt in the very pages of his masterwork. His poetic, culturally based vision of the age (which he had called "Kulturgeschichte") was so strong that it took scholarship more than a century to completely dislodge his hegemony over the field of Renaissance studies.[2]

We began that dislodgment by making connections that he never intended, letting ourselves into the private rooms which Burckhardt eschewed, interviewing the women, checking out the bedchambers. We rifled through private papers, tax forms, and visited the courtrooms and jails, expanding the dimensions of this historical time period of the Renaissance, dimensions that did not fit with his overall characterization of the age. What he had not emphasized of course were those elements that were invisible, or certainly not primary, for the elite and patriarchal European milieu of both his own and the Renaissance period. These were, namely, the lives of the lower classes, the dynamics of everyday economic life, the role of women in the culture—all still medieval in character. The society in which most people of the age lived was still hierarchical, ruled by oligarchy, and it operated from within the socioeconomic restrictions of traditional family ties. Yet even these new efforts to dislodge his hegemony took off from comments made by Burckhardt himself. The question was, should we move out or adapt?

In these pages, we will examine what Burckhardt *did* see in fifteenth-century Italy, and how subsequent generations of historians have filled in what he did *not* see. His had been a vision (what he called "Anschauung"), shaped in part by the age in which he lived and partially by his own creativity. He wrote that he was trying to capture the "clear signs of the time," and not the "mere facts," and in so doing, added another layer to the reinterpretation of the age which historians in the Renaissance had begun. Here I explore the idea that it was his coherent vision, focusing on the culture and grounded in the art produced in the Italian Renaissance, which created one of the most fertile areas for nineteenth- and twentieth-century historical scholarly endeavor. Based upon innovations he correctly identified among the elite, he developed and delivered a complete historical "package."

Burckhardt emphasized the creativity of the age; he showed the way in which entirely new artistic creations had emerged—for example, the State, the art of diplomacy, overseas exploration, Humanism, and finally, the modern notion of the individual. He gave many examples of the forms the State took, from despotism and dynasty to the republican states of Venice and Florence, seeing past their overt differences to their creative commonality. And it was in one of these states, namely Florence, that Burckhardt saw the fullest expression of the Renaissance inventions of Humanism and individualism.

Burckhardt himself was aware of the artistic license available to the historian in representing the past. He saw that the data of the past is multidimensional. Indeed, as Jacob Burckhardt wrote on the first page of his book, "to each eye, . . . the outlines of a given civilization present a different picture," and further,

> in the wide ocean upon which we venture, the possible ways and directions are many; and the same studies which have served for this work might easily, in other hands, not only receive a wholly different treatment and application, but lead also to essentially different conclusions.[3]

Here, I want to develop the notion that the continued reinvention of Renaissance studies, and specifically those centered on Florence, is due, firstly, to Burckhardt's broadly cultural approach, which proved to be poetically malleable for future generations of historians. What has made this historical vision useful and productive, and at the same time open to criticism, is precisely its straightforward admission of subjectivity (subsequently abhorred by post-Annales-School "social scientists"), which left the doors of inquiry and direction ajar. But secondly, it is what Burckhardt identified there in the Renaissance as *new*, namely the birth of modern individualism, which has made it so appealing and accommodating for subsequent generations of historians in the twentieth century, from political scholars to feminists.

The problems Burckhardt's work has created were partly his fault and, in part, not his own doing. For example, he himself did not adequately discuss the role of the arts in his book. His publisher, however, attempted to rectify this omission by appending to subsequent editions of the work a spectacular collection of Renaissance artwork; Renaissance images which were to serve as illustrations of Burckhardt's newly identified Renaissance individualism. This treatment of the art of the period thereby set up a dangerous precedent for the field of Renaissance studies. Generations of historians followed suit, often using the art generated during the Renaissance as simply illustrative, ancillary material, rather than as primary sources which were in fact not self-explanatory, but which needed to be subjected to the same historical criticism as written texts. I want to suggest here that this practice has not only been problematic, but may also have influenced the course of post-Burckhardtian scholarship.

BURCKHARDT'S BACKGROUND

Jacob Burckhardt was a Swiss Protestant historian with an interest in art, born in 1818 into an upper-class family of intellectuals and businessmen from the city of Basel. His father himself was trained in philosophy and theology and ministered to the oldest Protestant church in the city. He educated his son Jacob as the Renaissance Humanists themselves had been educated, in classical Latin and Greek literature, and provided enough family money for him to travel abroad to familiarize himself with the surviving architectural and artistic monuments of ancient Greece and Rome. In the summer of 1838, Jacob had journeyed to northern Italy, including Florence, and ten years later, during which the "People's Springtime" popular uprisings of 1848 caught him in Rome, was still a relatively young man of thirty.

By the age of forty-two, Burckhardt had read, travelled, and studied sufficiently to produce his own unique synthesis of previous French, German, and Italian thinking on the subject of the Renaissance. He befriended the young Nietzsche, and imbibed the philosophical ideas of both Schopenhauer and Hegel.[4] His masterwork predictably discussed the high culture of fifteenth-century Italy, that is, the culture of those men like himself in nineteenth-century Basel—upper-class, affluent, educated.

But Jacob was not simply a product of his times. He was a creative and independent thinker. While the earliest turbulence of emerging nationalistic tendencies was sweeping an increasingly industrialized northern Europe, Burckhardt himself resisted the lure of political involvement. He did not share in the enthusiasm shown by many of his close friends for the patriotic fervor of the newly-forming nation-states of the mid-nineteenth century. Instead, Burckhardt turned his attention to an earlier time (a time he perhaps saw as diametrically opposed to his own), a period in which old political entities were breaking up, in part allowing the first rugged individuals to emerge. As a Swiss Protestant, he seems to have been fascinated, as many of his interpreters have noted, with the "Otherness" of Renaissance Italy, its Roman Catholicism, its Mediterranean passions. There was a fervor to his descriptive prose which gave the lie to total objectivity, but in spite of this (or perhaps *because* of this), it drew historians into the study of the period he so evocatively presented.

Burckhardt as Creative Visionary

The Renaissance, as a Burckhardtian concept, has always evoked a mental image of an overriding vitality and color. Thanks to Burckhardt and to the Italian poets, artists, and historians themselves, visual images of this era can be called up perhaps more easily than of any other time in European history. Even though his vision has been widely criticized, no one would deny that it is still an overwhelmingly seductive construct; a candy store of vibrant images and personal vigor which we of the twentieth century have longed to recapture—to drag forward into our own fragmented and postmodern lives. There is a painterly consistency in his metanarrative which is still endlessly appealing.[5]

Thanks in great part to Burckhardt's book, the Renaissance conjures up for most people a picture of a series of great individual personalities, such as Leonardo da Vinci, Machiavelli, Michelangelo, Raphael; maybe even Boccaccio, Castiglione, Lorenzo de Medici, Savonarola, or Burckhardt's own quintessential Renaissance man, Leon Battista Alberti. Burckhardt wrote that Alberti had excelled in literature, architecture, riding, fencing, dancing, was a pioneer in the critical theory of art, and even gave his name to the figured bass line in music, the Alberti bass; all the while surviving outside the city of Florence as part of an exiled family of worth, by educating himself and then working as a lawyer attached to the Vatican (as protonotary), and a diplomat.[6] He used Alberti to create the image of the "Renaissance Man," a man universally gifted—the stuff of which legends are made.

Of course, not all the grand individuals of the age were of great moral worth, but Burckhardt does not eschew their discussion. Pope Alexander IV's son, the cruel and cunning Cesare Borgia, and the shrewd mercenary and later Duke of Milan, Francesco Sforza, are also included in his chapter on the development of the individual. He is simultaneously fascinated and repelled by the excesses of individual Renaissance personalities, but nevertheless celebrates their energetic egoism. He wrote of the conquering *condottiere* Francesco that perhaps he was "the man most after the heart of his age. Never was the triumph of genius and individual power more brilliantly displayed than in him . . ."[7]

What Burckhardt identified there in Renaissance Italy, and what was borne out in his studies, was also the first evidence of the desirability of personal fame (or glory), and the development of individual reputation among the Humanists. He writes,

> The new race of poet-scholars which arose soon after Dante quickly made themselves master of this fresh tendency [for fame]. They did so in a double sense, being themselves the most acknowledged celebrities of Italy, and at the same time, as poets and historians, consciously disposing of the reputation of others . . .[8]

The Renaissance, after Burckhardt, has been identified with the beginnings of Humanism, incorporating a new focus on mankind and the physical world, a turning away from the medieval model of mind with its more spiritual, otherworldly concerns, and toward active scholarly involvement to create a more vibrant and fulfilling life.

The author, however, initially does have difficulty characterizing these Renaissance Humanists, because his grand, nineteenth-century sweep of cultural perspective includes not only those cities where Humanists were chancellors in the employ of the State (such as Salutati and Bruni in Florence), but also those dynasties and despotisms, including the papacy itself, where Humanists walked a tenuous line between individual scholarship and enrichment on the one hand, and (where denied any real political opportunity) a certain amount of slavish fawning in the employ of the local prince on the other. He begins his characterization by writing,

> they were a crowd of the most miscellaneous sort, wearing one face today and another tomorrow; but they clearly felt themselves, and it was fully recognized by their time, that they formed a wholly new element in society. . . .[9]

But not to be thwarted by complexity, Burckhardt the historian continues on, determined to discover some sort of internal unity out of evident external diversity,

> they became influential because they knew what the ancients knew, because they tried to write as the ancients wrote, [and] because they began to think, and soon to feel, as the ancients thought and felt.[10]

It was not their political involvement then, which had created their individuality. It was their study of antiquity. Out of a plethora of individual facts he discerns, or is able to create, some sense of unity. His characterization of the Humanists has provided subsequent historians endless opportunities for further investigation.[11]

Burckhardt convinced himself of the importance of the Humanists as the catalytic element in Renaissance society, and went on to portray the rebirth of classical learning and the revival of antiquity through the exempla of Dante, Petrarch, and Boccaccio, three Florentines who most characterized this "new class of men," these "poet-scholars."[12] He described the fifteenth century in Florence, with its development of the discipline of philology (the science of the meaning and history of words) as the time of greatest brilliance, and used its citizens like Poggio as examples of the newly-empowered men. Burckhardt wrote almost longingly about the Florentines.

> That wondrous Florentine spirit, at once keenly critical and artistically creative, was incessantly transforming the social and political condition of the state, and as incessantly describing and judging the change.... The spectacle of ancient Rome and a familiarity with its leading writers were not without influence.... Florence obtained ... a greater fame than fell to the lot of any other city of Italy.[13]

Who among us interested in the history of ideas could resist his siren song to the study of Florence, which Burckhardt called, along with Venice, a city with "deep significance for the history of the human race!" Who would not be tempted to retrace the genesis of such significance, if for nothing more than to prove him wrong?[14]

Burckhardt also discussed the flowering of material culture, implicitly recognizing the fine arts of painting, sculpture, and architecture as its highest creation. Renaissance art, for him the central aspect of the "genius" of Italian culture, achieved technical mastery of realism in painting, beginning in the early 1300s with Giotto's freshly-natural frescoes in the Scrovegni Chapel in Padua. Interestingly enough, however, Burckhardt only *alluded* to the fine arts in his great masterwork as finally published. Instead, aiming for the jugular, Burckhardt gave us memorably sensual images of this period, writing that "even the outward appearance of men and women and the habits of daily life were more perfect, more beautiful, and more polished than among the other nations of Europe."[15] His prose created a utopian image of harmonious social intercourse, an image that proved peculiarly resonant for the restless modern world of the twentieth century. We are fascinated as we read,

> Outward life...was polished and ennobled as among no other people in the world. A countless number of those small things and great things which combine to make up what we mean by comfort, we know to have first appeared in Italy. In the well-paved streets of the Italian cities, driving was universal, while elsewhere

> in Europe walking or riding was the custom. . . . We read in the novelists of soft, elastic beds, of costly carpets and bedroom furniture . . . of the abundance and beauty of the linen . . . we note with admiration the thousand ways in which art ennobles luxury, . . .[16]

Since Burckhardt first pointed it out, we have been aware of the extent to which the glory of the Florentine state was a self-conscious creation of the Florentines themselves. Florentines, perhaps more desperately (and successfully) than the citizens of any other city-state, had wanted to control what posterity would see. They wanted to construct anew their own written and visual history. Thanks to Jacob Burckhardt, we know how they employed a newly revitalized study of antiquity, especially of Roman history, as the model for their state.

We are also aware, because of Burckhardt, that the upper-class Florentine oligarchs, using the study of the humanities (the *studia humanitatis*) to represent themselves to others, had created the convincing illusion that a new Roman republic had been revived in their late medieval city. Humanists in the employ of the commune such as Coluccio Salutati, Leonardo Bruni, and Bartolomeo Scala took up the banner of civic responsibility *all'antica* to embrace a new life of active engagement, abandoning the older medieval ideal of solitary withdrawal to a life of scholarly study and religious meditation. The vision they advanced of the Florentine state as a vigorous, secular democracy, even a meritocracy, where a shrewd young individual with a solid Humanist education could flourish, was as creative a societal construction as Europe had seen since antiquity.

In order to project this image, the Florentine Humanists employed by the commune had to rewrite historical accounts of the city; to establish new historical origins. Thus, Bruni, one of Burckhardt's "poet-historians," determined to prove that Florence had been founded during the revered ancient Republic—rather than during the despised Empire—as medieval historians, enamored of the Roman Empire, had asserted. He set out to discover the facts that would make his case, and was successful.[17]

Along with this new history, Burckhardt saw that the Florentines had to update new value systems and suit them to the new fashion. No longer, as in medieval times, did the celibate scholar have pride of place. Civic activism, family life, impeccable manners, physical prowess, economic and social involvement, and patronage of the plastic arts now needed to be factored in with erudition, to come up with the new ideal

Renaissance man. The modern social virtues of "grace under pressure" and "never let them see you sweat" were seen as having been born there in Florence.

BURCKHARDT AS ART HISTORIAN

As primarily an art historian interested in "Kultur," the fine arts had been, understandably, utmost in Burckhardt's interests. His masterwork presupposed some knowledge of the art of the period, and he had, in fact, originally intended his *Civilization of the Renaissance in Italy* to explore the cultural foundations of the art, with a second, companion volume planned to detail the artistic production itself. The second volume, however, never appeared, thus leaving his enduring vision to stand alone, essentially in an unfinished form.[18] What we do have on art within his book is a series of unconnected references to Renaissance artists as individual men, with no sustained or substantive discussion of the objects they created or the specific way in which they transformed the Renaissance culture, society, and urban environment. The spectacle of Brunelleschi's dome for the cathedral of Santa Maria del Fiore for example, is not here, but a reference to an obscure mechanical device invented by him for a Feast of the Annunciation celebration, is. None of Leonardo's paintings is mentioned, but his being on the payroll of the Duke of Milan until 1494, is.[19] Giants of Renaissance art such as Masaccio, Fra Angelico, Uccello, Mantegna, Veneziano, Piero della Francesca, and even Botticelli, Verrocchio and Tintoretto are absent from these pages, and in fact of the artists who do appear, about sixteen, more than half figure only in a brief one-sentence aside. Of those artists who are mentioned more than once, only Raphael and Michelangelo have their artworks referred to by name.[20]

More often, Burckhardt used artists to serve as examples of Renaissance people caught up, like others, in the cosmopolitan urban society of the day; employed by dukes and popes, and often underpaid. He quickly sketched a chaotic picture of artists incessantly travelling to work for patrons distant from their homes, and then, once employed, kept busy decorating rooms and designing entertainments and spectacles for their patrons. At the same time, these same artists are characterized as friends of writers, as the intimates of humanists and scholars, and in the case of Leonardo, as one of the geniuses of any age. The stature of some Renaissance artists is suggested, for example, by Lorenzo de Medici's asking the Spoletans to return the body of Florentine artist Fra Filippo Lippi, because the city needed such ornament. But we have no discussion of Lippi's artistic contribution.[21]

In other words, the art historian Jacob Burckhardt created a compellingly poetic and coherent cultural history of the Renaissance, *without* directly discussing the art, an omission that may have unintentionally misled later historians of the period. The illustrations of Renaissance figures that were included in subsequent editions of his masterwork after the initial publication were neither selected by Burckhardt himself nor were they a part of his original plan, but were later added by Ludwig Goldscheider, who worked for Burckhardt's publisher. These illustrations played a big part in popularizing Burckhardt's book, and also visually reinforced his basic assertion, that the Renaissance was the birthplace of individualism. Page after page of illustrations showed accomplished, famous men and women from this time period, such as Lorenzo de Medici, Ludovico "Il Moro" Sforza, Baldasssare Castiglione, Isabella d'Este, Caterina Cornaro, Leonardo da Vinci, Julius II. In fact, more than one-third of the 421 Renaissance images here were secular, individual portraits in paint, bronze, or stone. But these pictures have no direct references in Burckhardt's text. Without his own commentary on the artistic merit of these images, or on the *political* agenda for which the artists had created them, these faces became instead Renaissance "photos," direct visual "proof" of the existence of the newly-invigorated individuals Burckhardt had identified. Burckhardt himself would have known that these images had been commissioned by a new generation of secular art patrons, anxious to forward themselves in a certain light, but this discussion was *not* included in his book.

Instead, in his text, Burckhardt laid the sociocultural *base* for the fine arts, by broadening his definition of the term *art*, which he defined generally as a "product of reflection," and an "act of conscious creation."[22] By using this wider definition, Burckhardt introduced an enduring warfare, all became cultural "arts," arts that he believed laid the basis for the highest expression of the age in painting, sculpture and architecture.

CREATIVITY UNLEASHED: NEW DIRECTIONS

So Jacob Burckhardt viewed everything—statecraft, diplomacy, even war—as a manifestation of the artistic expression and creativity of this age, but did not discuss the art itself. By leaving out a substantive and sophisticated analysis of the political role played by Renaissance arts and artists, Burckhardt left us with an ambiguity about the art, with a malleable model, open for remodeling. While he did identify the greatest of the artists, namely, Leonardo, Michelangelo, and Raphael, as unique individuals (comparable to the Humanists)—as men able to rise above the political fray by dint of their individual "genius"—the vast majority of Renaissance artists who became caught up in portraying the political agendas of their patrons (such as Ghirlandaio, whom we will see below) are left unexamined. This created a false impression of the independence of the artists and, more importantly, of the images they crafted. By the time Burckhardt's book achieved classic status, other historians, especially historians of politics, were filling in the lacunae left by his book, but not in a way with which he would necessarily have agreed.

THE CREATION OF "CIVIC HUMANISM"

Although he was certainly correct in his vision of the centrality of artistic creativity in Renaissance life, Burckhardt did not make clear the fact that life in the cities was still, by and large, oligarchic—even in Florence. In reality, family lineage, connections, and money were the elements that still kept most men at the top, even there. Burckhardt himself had instead been interested in what was new about the period, and always separated Renaissance Humanist ideals from the gritty real world of oligarchic power. This nineteenth-century art historian, perhaps reacting against the centralizing tendencies in the emerging nationalism of his own age, was determined to demonstrate that these had been two discrete realms.

But for twentieth-century historians at midcentury whose major concern was politics (not art or cultural history), this separation came under pressure. For the twentieth century everything became a possible manifestation of politics. Working from within this major Burckhardtian theme, scholarly research began to establish a strong connection between Humanist culture and political power. It was Hans Baron's agenda-setting contribution, articulated in his book *The Crisis of the Early Italian Renaissance* in the mid-1950s, that first challenged one of Burckhardt's basic assertions.[23]

Baron agreed with Burckhardt that modern individualism had begun in Renaissance Florence, but disagreed about the genesis, about what had caused, that individualism. Burckhardt had postulated that the full realization of the individual was a result of Humanistic studies undertaken by men of means who stayed out of the political arena—at their leisure. Baron argued, conversely, that it was not from their leisure studies, but from their intense involvement in the self-governance of their own city that their individualism, their individual sense of self, had developed.

Further, Baron argued that the full honing of the doctrine of what he called "civic humanism" was in direct response to the political and military threat from the despotic Milanese to the north. Looking back to the 1950s, one can see that the very terminology Baron used for the tensions between Florence and Milan in the late fourteenth and early fifteenth centuries, was a melding of Burckhardtian Humanism, American individualism, and his own Cold War mentality.

What had convinced Baron that Burckhardt had been wrong, and that Humanism and politics in Florence had been intimately linked? Besides reading Bruni and Salutati, Baron (and others) could have noted the overwhelming visual evidence of Florentine Renaissance art—art such as Burckhardt's publisher had appended to Burckhardt's own book. For if we look back at the new intellectual direction, first taken by Florence under chancellor Salutati in the 1390s, we can see that its merchant elite had not simply been attempting to marry the humanistic "art" of statecraft with the reality of politics in their writing. They were also busy constructing a visual and architectural linkage.

Beginning in the early 1400s through secular patronage of the arts, especially by the corporations of the major guilds, art and politics were forged together. The political patronage of the arts fundamentally changed the look of the Florentine urban environment. If Florence wanted to be thought of as a new republican State, visual evidence of the

FIG. 5.1 Domenico Ghirlandaio, *Angel Appearing to Zacharias* (1486); Tornabuoni Chapel, Santa Maria Novella, Florence, Scala /Art Resource, N.Y.

FIG. 5.2 Domenico Ghirlandaio, *Birth of Saint John* (1486); Tornabuoni Chapel, Santa Maria Novella, Florence, Scala /Art Resource, N.Y.

FIG. 5.3 Domenico Ghirlandaio, Detal of Antonio Pucci, Lorenzo de' Medici, and Francesco Sassatti and his son, from *The Confirmation of the Rule* (1483–85); Sassetti Chapel, Santa Trinita, Florence, Scala /Art Resource, N.Y.

oligarchy would have to go (or at least become hidden behind the rusticated walls of private palazze). From narrow medieval lanes and cul-de-sacs shadowed by the towers of the *magnati*, the oligarchs of Florence opened up public space through ironically merciless urban renewal projects that created elegant large piazze (Santa Maria Novella, Santa Croce, Santa Maria del Fiore, the Piazza della Signoria), suitable for official processions, the arrival of foreign diplomats, Latin oratory, and the display of republican crowds composed of the Florentine citizenry. This merchant elite paid the architect Brunelleschi, for example, to dome the cathedral in spectacular classical fashion by 1430. Likewise, they hired

Ghiberti to adorn the doors of the Baptistery in gold relief, portraying Biblical stories in classical settings. Newly commissioned architectural and sculptural triumphs such as Brunelleschi's design for the foundling hospital, the Ospedale degli Innocenti, and the free-standing, larger-than-life heroic statues (including Donatello's Saint Mark) in niches around Or San Michele (the old grain market and commercial center of the Commune), now added antique dignity and purpose to urban life—a certain republican aura.[24]

For a twentieth-century historian primarily interested in Renaissance political life but also seeing this self-evident physical transformation, it would have been obvious that the commune of Florence had marshalled Humanistic values into State service during this era. Within his own book, Baron used three renderings of the city of Florence as illustrative of a change in the visual conception of the city between 1352 and 1493—a change he linked to Leonardo Bruni's early Quattrocento text, the *Laudatio Florentinae Urbis*, a hymn of praise for Florence.[25] Baron paraphrased Bruni's description of the city as "dominated by the Palazzo Vecchio, visible embodiment of central power . . . a mighty castle," which in turn is surrounded by the city itself. Outside the city proper, which is "ringed by walls and suburbs . . . lies a belt of rural mansions and estates and around them a circle of towns . . ."[26] Baron then compares Bruni's detailed description with one of the three renderings he includes, an image from the 1480s in which he sees "the same convergence of . . . a towering central 'castle,' the same successive 'rings' of city fortifications, suburbs, hill towns . . ." and the like.[27]

This is one instance of how the art and architecture produced at this time within Florence seems to have influenced twentieth-century historians. Art is often seen as illustrative of the historian's own perceptions, in the same way that Burckhardt's publisher had illustrated *his* point (the emergence of individualism), some one hundred years earlier. Baron comments that the 1480s image in his book shows a Humanist interest "in mathematical rule and the natural order of things."[28] While the image is interesting in its visual correspondence to Bruni's text, it neither intrinsically supports nor denies Baron's thesis of the existence of a developmental link between Florentine Humanist thought and Humanist political involvement in the Commune. Without knowledge of *why* this image was made, who commissioned it, or what purpose this image was to fulfill, we cannot intelligently assess its historical meaning. My aim here is not to question Baron's revision of Burckhardt, but merely to point out that the historical use of the artwork of this period also has its antecedents in Burckhardt's book itself.

Linking Art with Politics

But back to the Florence of the Renaissance. The Florentine state, then, was not only conceived by the Humanist elite as a reborn, morally prosperous republican Rome, but also rebuilt and eventually represented by painters, sculptors, and architects employed by the same elite, to preserve for themselves, their families, and for posterity, the images of this idealized city-state. A fifteenth-century legend was in the making.

One relatively minor Florentine artist, who has since been identified as an excellent example of this marriage of art and statecraft in Florence, is the painter Domenico Ghirlandaio (1449–1494). He, among many, was commissioned essentially to convey the new vision of Florentine statehood. His contributions, however, have never been considered the highest expression of visionary talent in the Quattrocento, paling before such greater artistic lights as Michelangelo or Raphael. In fact, art historians of the twentieth century have consistently seen in Ghirlandaio a certain fussiness and specificity characteristic of the age, an attention to detail in portraiture, dress, and interior design that has excluded him from the timelessness requisite of, say, a Leonardo. They have not seen in his work the central theme of the newly-embraced classical values which he was actually hired to depict.

His art has been recently described (here and in Italy) as simply illustrative of the "reality" of the fifteenth-century Florentine republic, rather than as the production of an artist attempting to satisfy his clients' own visions of themselves, their families, and their social place in the ideal republican state. However, it is this reading of the art of Ghirlandaio as mere fifteenth-century illustrator that has made him so important for the subsequent development of Florentine historiography. Italian art historian Micheletti gave voice to this naive assessment of Ghirlandaio's work, writing,

> It must be stated again that over and above any assertion about the ease and absolute mastery of his art . . . Domenico Ghirlandaio is the most complete, pleasing and *faithful illustrator* of this society in perhaps the most splendid period of the city, which he brings back to life almost day by day in its characters, its streets and palaces, in the very atmosphere which surrounds them . . .[29] (my emphasis)

The artistic representation of the ideal Humanist republic, which Micheletti here described as fifteenth-century reality, can be briefly shown by examples from two elaborate fresco cycles completed by Ghirlandaio and his assistants in the mid-to-late 1480s. Francesco Sassetti paid for the first of these fresco programs for his family chapel in the church of Santa Trinità, asking that the subject matter be the life of his name saint, Francis of Assisi. Giovanni Tornabuoni commissioned the second fresco for his family chapel in Santa Maria Novella, choosing as its subject the lives of the Virgin and Saint John the Baptist, the patron saint of Florence. Both patron-donors were Medici adherents and, as such, part of the inner circle of the Florentine merchant elite.

Besides providing the donors of these religious artworks with grace for their immortal souls, these depictions of scenes from the lives of saints each contained a contemporary secular component, for both fresco cycles included full-length portraits of members of the wealthy and influential Tornabuoni and Sassetti families, along with their circles of "parenti, amici e vicini"—that is, their relatives, friends and neighbors—arranged in the foreground of the many scenes (fig. 5.1). Some of the people pictured in these frescoes can be identified without question, the identity of others has been extrapolated from extant written documents, and others still are in the process of being researched.[30] Late-twentieth-century historians of Florence can now read a definite political agenda in the way in which these frescoes were painted, an agenda that was perhaps not so fully studied some forty or fifty years ago.

For example, in the various panels from these two fresco cycles, there are stylistic differences in the way the genders are portrayed. The young, nubile women of the families are posed as icons of communal wealth, symbols of republican prosperity. They are shown standing alone, isolated figures dressed to the nines in brocades, velvets, and jewels. They are separated from the males of their families so as not to contaminate them with their individual display of wealth (fig. 5.2).

The men of the families and their male cohorts, by way of contrast, are arranged together in such a way as to suggest a certain elegant egalitarianism to the male groups; an egalitarian look the oligarchs of Florence were eager to advance. Even the unofficial political and cultural head of Florence, Lorenzo "Il Magnifico" de' Medici appears. He stands between two other men, plainly (and elegantly) dressed but no different from the others, *primus inter pares*, that is, first among equals (fig. 5.3). Echoes of republican Rome among the men are made visually manifest.

It is not difficult to see why this early Florentine Renaissance resonated so well both with contemporary concerns and twentieth-century scholarship. Modern historians saw in these self-representations the spirit of an energetic community, democratic republicanism, a sense of opportunity, a work ethic, a fluid social structure, a secular approach to life, and above all, easy rationale of the necessity of wealth (on the backs of the women).[31] All this spoke to us, reminded us of our own idealized selves.

The art of Ghirlandaio, and others who painted secular pictures for the merchant elite, seemed to bear out modern, twentieth-century qualities in the Florentines of the fifteenth century. No effeminate foppish dress like the dandies of Siena for the restrained "molto raffinato" citizens of Florence. These were family men, men whose wives upheld the familial spirituality and Christian moral code, and passed it on to the children, while still looking fabulous! These were not celibate ascetics, but family men, active in city politics, whose greatest concern was to educate their sons and marry their daughters well, bringing new blood (and infusions of cash, if possible) into the family line. We could relate to them.[32]

Historians who sought visualizations of Florence now can see that Ghirlandaio was not simply mirroring "reality," for the republican look he represented did not *exist* in reality. After decades of archival work, transcribing tax records, inventories, and communal sumptuary legislation, we know now that it was staged. In the case of Ghirlandaio, we know about the ornate jewelry and clothes which the men he painted actually had in their closets and presumably wore, when they were not posing in plain robes of muted scarlet for republican posterity.

That this representation should have once been read as anything approaching an "objective" rendering of the Florentine state, is indicative of the way in which, for better or worse, generations of historians have been shaped by Burckhardt's work and its inherent ambiguities.[33] The title of Baron's last work, *In Search of Florentine Civic Humanism*, is an eloquent testament to the enduring power of the agenda that the Florentines themselves wanted to advance. The search for the Florentine ideal goes on. Historians have developed a sophisticated skepticism with which to read written primary sources, and some of us are now directing this same skepticism to visual images from the era of the Renaissance.

BURCKHARDT EXPANDED

Just as Burckhardt found nineteenth-century issues resonant in fifteenth-century Florence, just as he identified with the Humanists of Florence, so today, historians in the United States have found twentieth-century American issues imbedded there. Not only Burckhardt, but his heirs like Baron, and probably all historians of every age, reflect the concerns of their own era.

Even before Baron had revised Burckhardt's conclusions on Humanism, early twentieth-century historians in other areas of study had begun to incorporate new developments in European historiography, especially those of the early *Annales* School in France. The "Annalistes" argued for a more inclusive, more "objective" and "scientific" method of studying the past.[34] However, the social-science approach was slow to catch on in Renaissance studies, which still worked for the most part from within the commodious cultural approach that Burckhardt had constructed, based on the arts.

It was not until the 1960s that the field of social history finally was successful in challenging Burckhardt's hegemony in the field.[35] Twentieth-century concerns about class polarization, the increasing focus on gender studies, labor, the poor and marginalized—made Burckhardt's elite cultural approach to the Renaissance seem out-of-touch and unpalatable. Thus, the new social historians, many of whom were Marxists, only mentioned him in the opening remarks of their books. Now, instead of Burckhardt, footnotes teemed with references to other nineteenth and early twentieth-century Italian historians who had focused on specific socioeconomic problems of the period.[36]

In the subsequent decades, Renaissance historiography has finally embraced demographic approaches to its subject, incorporating aspects of *Annales'* call for sociological models. But these very avenues had been noted by Burckhardt himself. Within his masterwork, he had first discussed the Renaissance cities of Florence and Venice as the "birthplace of statistics," due to their natural propensity for the "systematization of outward life."[37]

But Burckhardt's cultural approach increasingly came under fire for its omissions, and in fact, in history departments throughout the United States, the designation "Renaissance" was often seen as an invalid title for this period of history. Students either studied "late medieval" or "early modern" history, with "Renaissance" seen as an art-historical designation. In their eyes, Burckhardt's focus on the arts, which did not provide definitive proof of the transformation of societal institutions, demonstrated that the "Renaissance" was not, in fact, a discrete historical period. It belonged, ironically enough, only to the realm of art history.

And finally, Burckhardt's cultural slight to women undoubtedly fanned into flames feminist scholarship of the Renaissance. His by-now infamous remark that women "stood on a footing of perfect equality with men" during this period was answered in the 1970s by Joan Kelley's now equally-famous article which memorably asked if women even *had* a Renaissance.[38] We still wish to see women somehow truly acknowledged in this period, however, a period which, with Burckhardt's help, has been so fundamental to the discussion of the genesis of Western consciousness. Historians now know that Burckhardt's comments on women were themselves erroneous, and only referred to the exceptional women of the elite. We know that he was in error when he opined that

> we must not suffer ourselves to be misled by the sophistical and often malicious talk about the assumed inferiority of the female sex . . . by such [men] as Ariosto, who treats woman as a dangerous grown-up child, whom a man must learn how to manage . . .[39]

We realize that Ariosto's misogynistic point-of-view was simply a commonplace about women during this period.

But we still take notice of the occasional Renaissance feminist comment, when it surfaces. For example, in Lauro Martines' new book, *An Italian Renaissance Sextet*, he discusses a short story by Lorenzo de' Medici, and comments on Lorenzo's "startling" statement regarding women. Lorenzo had written,

> women's misfortune seems to me to be a great one, . . . since no matter how insignificant and pathetic a man may be, when he takes a wife, he always wishes to choose one who pleases him, or not take her at all; whereas a woman, without knowing what or why is subject to the wishes of others and must take what is given to her in order not to have worse.[40]

The short story in which this statement appears is rife with fifteenth-century misogynist attitudes of the day—female sexual insatiability, cunning, even propensity for blasphemy—but Lorenzo's passing, modern-sounding feminist statement is noted by the late twentieth-century historian. It is what the historian's eye picks out and highlights. It is this statement which stays with us and will be quoted long after the short story is forgotten; a trace of the modern in this still overwhelmingly traditional, fifteenth-century society that we want to relate to, to even marvel at; those glimmerings of the *new* that provide the links into future consciousness.

CONCLUSIONS

Poetic historical constructs give meaning and shape to the past and provide coherent metanarratives for its study. Thanks to Jacob Burckhardt's sociocultural approach to the history of the Italian Renaissance, we continue to find ourselves there, in this first period of modernity. His sweeping construction of a broadly inclusive definition of art, including the creation of the State, of diplomacy, of individualism, Humanism and even war, created a breadth of vision in which we felt included. We saw modern similarities, points of tangency, nodes of concern, even as his omission of the plastic arts, for which this period is known, created continuing confusion and ambiguity.

With his initial construction, the palazzo of the mind built in the 1860s, now alternately ignored, revised, or despised—but still standing out there in the distance—we continue to want to find ourselves there in that period, to find individual glory, human power, rewards for our labor. But the vision and the legends of the poet-historians must be continually updated by current consciousness. Floors sag and the roof is leaking. Some of the unused rooms are filling up with spiders. Can we, as modern historians, continue to find accommodation within his sweeping nineteenth-century construction, or do we move? I, for one, am giving his house historical designation, and building a new one of my own in the suburbs.

Notes

1. Jacob Burckhardt, *The Civilization of the Renaissance in Italy*, trans. S. G. C. Middlemore (London: Penguin Classics, 1990).

2. Petrarch himself never used the Latin verb *rinascor* ("to be reborn") in his writing to refer to the resurgence of interest in ancient literature which he helped to lead in the mid-1300s. Rather, art historian Giorgio Vasari (1511–74) later coined the noun *renaissance* (in Italian, *rinascità*). But the application of the French term *Renaissance* to characterize the late-fourteenth through early-sixteenth century period, was first traced by the early twentieth-century historian Huizinga to a descriptive phrase in Balzac's 1829 novel *Le Bal de Sceau*. Michelet then used this term as the title of his book *La Renaissance* in 1855, just five years before Burckhardt's *Die Kultur der Renaissance in Italien* first appeared in German in 1860. See Erwin Panofsky for this history of the terminology in *Renaissance and Renascences in Western Art* (New York: Harper & Row, 1972), 5, n.1.

See also Wallace Ferguson's definitive study of the changing interpretations of the Renaissance in his book, *The Renaissance in Historical Thought* (Boston: Houghton Mifflin Co., 1948), 159–252.

3. Jacob Burckhardt, *The Civilization of the Renaissance in Italy*, 19.

4. See Peter Burke's introduction to the 1990 edition of Burckhardt's book, 3, 11.

5. See Hans Baron's two-volume work of 1988, which identifies subsequent diverging views of this period, one giving hegemony to French culture, and the other, identifying the developments in Italy in this period as a localized phenomenon, not pointing the way to a generalized, European-wide "modern age." See Baron, *In Search of Florentine Civic Humanism* (Princeton: Princeton University Press, 1989), vol.II, 164–67.

6. Burckhardt, *Civilization*, 74.

7. Ibid., 43.

8. Ibid., 76, in his chapter, "The Development of the Individual."

9. Ibid., 136.

10. Loc. cit.

11. For an updated bibliography of work on Humanist thought (and related areas) through the 1980s, see Lauro Martines, *Power and Imagination* (Baltimore: Johns Hopkins University Press, 1990), in his extensive supplementary bibliography, 353–56.

12. Ibid., 104–10.

13. Loc. cit. He goes on to recall that it was a Florentine, Giovanni Villani, who "received the first impulse to his great work" (his chronicle of the history of Florence), "at the jubilee of the year 1300, and began it immediately on his return home." But as Burckhardt further notes, ". . . how many among the 200,000 pilgrims of that year [in Rome] may have been like him in gifts and tendencies and still did not write the history of their native cities!" This quality of energetic industry, for Burckhardt, separated the Florentines from the rest; elevated them to Humanistic hegemony.

14. Ibid., 57.

15. Ibid., 236, from the section on everyday life, entitled "Society and Festivals."

16. Ibid., 239.

17. Leonardo Bruni's 1415 *Histories of the Florentine People*, originally composed in Latin, is probably the best example of the historiography written to accommodate this new vision. Leonardo Bruni, *Historiae Florentini Populi*, in *Rerum Italicarum Scriptores*, ed. Lodovico Muratori (Bologna: N. Zanichelli, 1926), vol. 19, pt. 3.

18. The intended volume on the art never appeared. Instead, a study of the architecture of the Renaissance was published in 1867, in German. But by 1878, the first English translation of his masterwork had already appeared, and was then translated into French, Polish, and Italian by the early 1900s. Burckhardt's book has gone through seven editions in English and innumerable reprints since then, establishing itself as a literary icon of historiography, all without any substantive discussion of his underlying assumption, namely, that Renaissance artistic production was, in his view, the finest fruit of the culture of that era. See Peter Burke's introduction to Burckhardt, 12.

19. Burckhardt, *Civilization*. For Brunelleschi see 260, 263; for the Leonardo reference, 45.

20. Ibid., for Raphael, see 38, 248, 267 and 329; for Michelangelo, 56, 118.

21. Ibid., 106.

22. Ibid., 79.

23. Hans Baron, *The Crisis of the Early Italian Renaissance*, 2 vols. (Princeton: Princeton University Press, 1955).

24. Frederick Hartt's *History of Italian Renaissance Art*, 3rd ed. (New York: Abrams, 1987), 141–77, is the current classic overview of these early Quattrocento artistic achievements.

25. Baron, *The Crisis*. For the renderings, see vol. 1, between 162–63. Bruni's *Laudatio* had used as its model Aristides' late Greek panegyric on the city of Athens. But whereas Aristides had been content to eulogize Athens abstractly, situating it, as Baron tells us, between "the disadvantages of plain and mountain-steepness, and between the extremes of climate," Bruni the Humanist was more specific, describing the physicality of Florence in rational detail. See 163–67.

26. Ibid., 167, 170.

27. Ibid., 171–173. Baron then contrasts this 1480s image with a second image, a mural painting from 1352 from the Loggia del Bigallo, which showed Florence with buildings that "still cluster in the medieval manner around an invisible center," and a third later image from 1493, created by a visiting German artist named Hartmann Schedel, in his *Liber chronicarum*, which displays "the late medieval pleasure in details without accents and distinctive order . . ." Whereas Baron sees a medieval commonality between the 1352 and the (northern) 1493 images then, the Florentine image of the 1480s, demonstrates to him a distinctly Humanist look, comparable to Bruni's *Laudatio*.

28. Ibid., 172.

29. Emma Micheletti, *Domenico Ghirlandaio* (London: Antella Scala, 1990), 60–61.

30. The definitive work on the conflict between Sassetti, Tornabuoni, and Lorenzo de' Medici is Eve Borsook and Johannes Offerhaus, *Sassetti and Ghirlandaio at Santa Trinita, Florence* (Holland: Davaco Publishers, 1981); see also work in progress by Rab Hatfield on Giovanni Tornabuoni's program in Santa Maria Novella.

31. The ongoing dispute among Florentine clerics, poets, and intellectuals regarding the amassing of money seems to have finally been put to rest by Bruni in the early Quattrocento in his statements about one needing wealth in order to be a valuable, contributing, alms-giving, arts-patronizing member of the community! See Baron's early article, "Franciscan Poverty and Civic Wealth" of 1938, discussed in Najemy's review article of Baron's newest book, *In Search of Florentine Civic Humanism*, in *Renaissance Quarterly* XLV, 2 (Summer 1992): 340–350.

32. We still use the energetic, poetically constructed paradigms of the legacy of Burckhardt's Renaissance to inform our value system today. Family, civic involvement, the worth of the community, liberal education, public eloquence, proper modes of behavior, the concept of "good taste," and even modern situational ethics (after Machiavelli), were all values first created by the

Humanist leadership of fifteenth-century Florence. They have become part of our lives, part of the Western tradition.

33. (But since his companion volume on Renaissance art never materialized, we do not know!) Baron, *In Search of*, op. cit.

34. In criticism of the more traditional narrative history, sociologists François Simiand and Emile Durkheim believed that history needed to be able not only to describe, but to explain. These early exponents of the scientific approach to history were persuaded that the individual could be understood solely from within the context of his or her own society, manifest in concrete. These institutional and material remains would then be the proper focus of historical investigation. With this Burckhardt would not have wholesalely disagreed.

But Simiand and Durkheim went on to argue that this study would not be enough. It would also need a methodology with laws, rules, and corollaries. It needed, in other words, a nomological approach that could construct a societal model. Then from such a model, hypothesis, analysis, and synthesis would be possible. Burckhardt's passion for uncovering the unique "genius" of an age would have dismissed the usefulness of such an overarching structure. See the discussion of their sociological approach to history in Georg G. Iggers, *New Directions in European Historiography*, 2nd ed. (Middletown, Conn.: Wesleyan University Press, 1984), especially 43–53.

35. For example, Roberto Lopez put forth a strikingly different picture of Renaissance Italy in his economic revisionist thesis of 1952. He believed that the Renaissance, in spite of Burckhardt's relentlessly vital, energetic, and upbeat picture of the period, with all its art patronage and building programs, had been a time of economic downturn and even depression. For this direct body blow to Burckhardt's vision, see Robert S. Lopez, "Hard Times and Investment in Culture," in *The Renaissance, A Symposium* February 8–10, 1952 (New York: Metropolitan Museum of Art, 1953); followed by Lopez and H.A. Miskimin, "The Economic Depression of the Renaissance," *Economic History Review* 14 (1962): 408ff. This controversy is still brewing. See Judith Brown's 1990 contribution "Prosperity or Hard Times in Italy?" *Renaissance Quarterly* XLIV, 4 (Winter, 1989): 761–780.

See also the seminal work done in 1963 by Lauro Martines, *The Social World of the Florentine Humanists 1390–1460* (Princeton: Princeton University Press, 1963), which established a socioeconomic reality for the literary personalities of Renaissance Humanists.

36. Among those cited during this time of social crisis were the Italians Salvemini, Fiumi, Rodolico, and Sapori; the Germans Davidsohn and Doren.

37. Burckhardt, *Civilization*, 63–69.

38. Ibid., 250–253. See Joan Kelley's "Did Women Have A Renaissance?" in *Becoming Visible*, ed. Renate Bridenthal, Claudia Koonz, and Susan Stuard, 2nd ed. (Boston: Houghton Mufflin, 1987), 175–201.

39. Burckhardt, *Civilization*, 250.

40. Martines then goes on to note that men of Lorenzo's social rank were also limited and bound by similar constraints in marriage choice, but did have access to extramarital consolations which were denied their sisters. Lauro Martines, *An Italian Renaissance Sextet: Six Tales in Historical Context* (New York: Marsilio, 1994), 162–163. This quote was taken from Lorenzo's short story ("*novella*") entitled *Giacoppo*, composed for circulation among a small circle of friends in the late 1460s.

CONTRIBUTORS

STEPHEN BROWN is a musician who studied art history at Harvard. He is author of *The Sense of Music* (Harcourt Brace Jovanovich, 1988), and has written a number of articles on David's revolutionary paintings.

CAROLE COLLIER FRICK is Associate Professor in the Department of Historical Studies at Southern Illinois University at Edwardsville, and has published articles on gender, class, and culture in Renaissance Italy.

EDMUND E. JACOBITTI is Professor Emeritus of History at Southern Illinois University at Edwardsville. He is author of *Revolutionary Humanism and Historicism in Modern Italy* (Yale University Press, 1981), and of numerous articles on European intellectual history.

JACQUELINE LEBLANC teaches at the Laboratory Institute of Merchandising in New York City. Her work on Shelley is part of a longer project examining aesthetics as political praxis in British Romantic writers. Her publications include "Politics and Commercial Sensibility in Helen Maria Williams' *Letters From France*," *Eighteenth Century Life*, (February, 1997), and " 'It is not good to note this down': *Dracula* and the Erotic Technologies of Censorship," in *Bram Stoker's* Dracula: *A Centenary Collection*, ed. Carol Margaret Davison (Oxford: Dundurn Press, 1997).

JOHN S. NELSON professes politics and communication at the University of Iowa, where he also assists with the Bridging Project on International Studies, and the Project on Rhetoric of Inquiry. His most recent book is *Tropes of Politics* (University of Wisconsin Press, 1998).

DAVID W. PRICE teaches English and comparative literature at Keene State College. He is author of *History Made, History Imagined* (University of Illinois Press, 1999), and numerous articles on writers such as Hegel, Diderot, Baudrillard, Salman Rushdie, Marguerite Yourcenar, and Christa Wolf, among others.

Index